Equal but Different

Equal but Different

The Transforming Power of Complementarity
in the Relationship Between Men and Women

Paul Dennis Sporer

QUENSTEDT PRESS

ANZA PUBLISHING, Chester, New York

Quenstedt Press is an imprint of Anza Publishing

Copyright © 2010 by Paul Dennis Sporer

Library of Congress Cataloguing-in-Publication Data
Sporer, Paul D.
  Equal but different / Paul Dennis Sporer.
    p. cm.
  Includes bibliographical references and index.
  Summary: "This book examines the mechanisms that men and women use to assess, interpret, and modify gender-connected personality traits, and how the similarities and differences in these traits affect the processes of courtship and married life"--Provided by publisher.
  ISBN 978–1–932490–35–0 (alk. paper)
  1. Man–woman relationships. 2. Marriage. 3. Men—Psychology. 4. Women—Psychology. 5. Sex differences (Psychology) I. Title.
  HQ801.S73 2010
  306.8101—dc22   2010051131

Visit AnzaPublishing.com for more information on outstanding authors and titles. Please support our efforts to restore great literature to a place of prominence in our culture.

ISBN-13: 978–1–932490–35–0 (softcover)

∞ This book is printed on acid-free paper.

To my dearest Cassandra

CONTENTS

Chapter 1
Introduction   1

Chapter 2
The Issue of Personality   13

Chapter 3
Opinions About Us   21

Chapter 4
Preserving Harmony   35

Chapter 5
Modern Simplifications   47

Chapter 6
The Narrowing of Married Life   58

Chapter 7
The Change in the Ideal   74

Chapter 8
Conclusions   90

Notes   *105*
References   *117*
Index   *123*

Idem velle atque idem nolle, ea demum firma amicitia est.
To have the same likes and dislikes—this, after all, is what
defines solid friendship.

    C. Sallustius Crispus (86–35 BC)

*Quae volumus et credimus libenter, et quae sentimus ipsi,
reliquos sentire speramus.*
What we desire, we readily believe, and what we ourselves
think, we expect others to think.

    C. Iulius Caesar (100–44 BC)

*Utinam lex esset eadem quae uxori est viro;
nam uxor contenta est, quae bona est, uno viro;
qui minus vir una uxore contentus siet?*
I wish there were the same rule for the husband and the wife.
Now a wife, a good wife, is content with just her husband;
why should a husband be less content with just his wife?

    Titus Maccius Plautus (c 255–184 BC)

*Ubi idem et maximus et honestissimus amor est, aliquanto
praestat morte iungi quam vita distrahi.*
When reciprocal love is very strong and very true, it is far
preferable to be joined in death, than parted in life.

    Valerius Maximus (fl c AD 30)

Chapter 1

Introduction

*I*ntelligent and astute men and women, by virtue of superior insight, spontaneously seek to accomplish what is beyond the visible and ordinary, for they struggle to reach the transcendent. They seek to utilise their natural desires to transform a situation by constructing the *apotheosis*, that is, the perfect example, the quintessence. Because of this, the natural desire for companionship, which is experienced by everyone, is raised to an ideal, by a few: Two people become one, through the interlocking of each person's unique qualities. Although material issues are important in establishing an enduring, close relationship, the desire to enjoy emotional gratification through contact with someone else has always been, and always will be, a preeminent factor. Yet, the fulfilment of this need requires the cooperation of another person. The individual must find ways to join all the components of relationship together, the self-enhancing with other-enhancing, the present with the future.

The strong motivation to have other people demonstrate affection, concern, and compassion towards oneself, begins in childhood and finds expression with parents, siblings, and relatives. Research on family life (Sporer 2010A, 2010B, 2010C), has made it clear that it is a universal attribute of the human persona to place a high premium on certain needs—the desire to be understood and recognised, to be advised and comforted. However, this ubiquitous concept of love does not entail, in its earliest immature phase, the equal share of responsibilities; it is self-centred, only concerned with receiving, and not giving in return. Children want to be loved, but their concept is that of support, their weakness is compensated by the strength of the parent. Further, this immaturity can extend into adulthood, and the psychological need to have an intimate relationship with the opposite sex cannot be completely reconciled with other life plans. Factors unrelated to the pertinent aspects of the relationship can actually become the motivating ingredients for marriage. It is therefore critical that this undeveloped aspect be magnified into a desire for *mutual love within a permanent relationship*. Only through significant social processes can this great goal be accomplished.

Thus, there can be no possibility of a transforming relationship unless there is an understanding of human interaction. From the earliest civilisation, man has had the strongest inquisitive interest to understand human motivations, for without this information about another person's opinions, attitudes, beliefs, there can be no secure friendship, no comradery, no amity. Knowledge must be gained from various sources, either from history or through commentary, that would facilitate the development of a compassionate awareness of the needs of others, and an ability to help others reach reasonable productive goals. All the great men of outstanding intellect and knowledge, from the time of the Bible onwards, have sought to add to this knowledge. Some of the greatest philosophers who have lived on the European continent have devoted their considerable mental resources to understanding the wide variety of components that operate in the psyche, and that potentially could have a substantive impact on human relations.

Indeed, European society has integrated much wisdom into its various cultures, providing advice, guidance, and boundaries in the realisation of emotional desires. Europeans have conceptualised the apotheosis of friendship as essentially two halves to a whole, which fulfills the purpose of *mutuality*, of equal energies being expended in serving the other, so that there is benefit for both through synergy. Such a relationship has been given the name of 'intimate love', and is synonymous with the fulfilment of the deepest desires.

We can see that the desire for mutual love, where the man wants to love a woman, but he also wants her to love him in return, is a sign of advancement, civility, and sophistication. In fact, there are few other desires in the human nature that so strongly express in a direct way a person's spirituality. Yet, such high development is all too infrequent. Oftentimes, we hear a husband might say 'I love my wife', but he does not really love her, because he married her *to be loved*, not necessarily because there was the possibility of experiencing mutual love. If this husband does not receive the sympathy and favour he expected from his spouse, then he considers the marriage to be a failure. However, the marriage was never genuine to begin with, since he did not make any attempt to love her the way he expected his wife to love him. The husband will now seek 'love' with other people; he does not believe he is unfaithful, since the marital relationship is, in his eyes, without value: There is nothing to cherish or protect.

Consequently, commensurate with the ideal of love is the concept of *wholeness*, which is often expressed in terms of family life; a married man says that he feels 'complete' because, with his spouse, he has arranged the affairs of life so that there is steadiness in purpose, as well as mental and emotional advancement. However, if the ideal is *defective*, then the absence of wholeness will motivate people, not to build and repair, but to abandon and destroy. If 'love' cannot be found in the family, then people will search for it elsewhere, sometimes to their own and another's detriment.

Despite the voluminous literature on marriage and family, virtually nothing has been written about this most important subject. Thus, we will endeavour to examine these themes in greater detail through the analyses in this work, so the methods that are used to create the 'interlocking' of attributes are revealed. Only in this way can one understand the true nature of the 'transformed' male-female relationship. We can say that numerous devices have been emplaced by European societies over the centuries that firstly, make men and women aware of the apotheosis of the relationship, and secondly, that can assist men and women in reaching the apotheosis. Further, we shall also examine the changes in the methods of assessment of personality traits, especially the inability of modern society to effectively utilise these methods, and how these changes have impacted the creation and maintenance of intimate relationships.

There are terms which we will use that efficiently describe personality comparisons. We can refer to a substantive likeness or similarity in a trait, belief or attitude as a *homology*, and the satisfaction that arises from the matching of ideas as *homophily*. In reference to substantive differences between two people, the term would be *heterology*, and for the positive emotional response to such a difference is *heterophily*. On this ground, we can say that *X*, a trait, belief, or attitude found in one partner and not the other, is a heterology, whilst the *attraction* that exists between these partners because of this incongruence is *heterophilic*. Further, we can say use the term *homology* or *heterology* to describe whether the overall set of traits, beliefs, and attitudes between two people are, in the main, similar or dissimilar, respectively.

Let us start by acknowledging that an intimate relationship between a man and woman contains all the same functions as an ordinary 'dyadic' friendship, including factors that control distance, support, and advice. People therefore determine the 'usefulness' of other people by evaluating them according to the most basic intellectual principle: Cataloguing *similarities and differences*. One holds up the mirror to view one's own personality, and then puts it down to see how others compare. The fundamental principles underlying the need for emotional gratification are present in the relationship between any two persons, regardless of gender. Traits are assigned a value, and are incorporated into the overall perception of the 'character' of the other person. However, the *priority* or order of these traits depends on the type of relationship. Certain traits are more important in intimate relationships compared to casual friendship, because there is greater investment of resources in the former.

The Greek philosopher Democritus stated that 'Similarity of mind makes friendship', and there is ample evidence from various cultures attesting to this principle as a major factor in interpersonal attraction. The principle can be summarised by using the oft-used but accurate expression: 'Like attracts like'. In fact, many societies encourage homology. Primitive societies often restrict marriage to within classes, whereas moderately advanced societies control various social gatherings as part of mate-choosing mechanisms, and the most sophisticated cultures, whilst not denying the importance of interpersonal differences, use informal procedures that reduce the likelihood of marriages that might be too dissimilar.[1] These customs reflect a collective interest in reducing the pool of potential candidates to those who have a background similar to oneself.

There are also many advantages in having two people who are substantively similar, as there are many areas where homology provides a *supportive* function. Similarity in basic habits creates a *mutual understanding* and an *ease of doing*. At the simplest level, communication can also be greatly facilitated when terms, metaphors, and ideas are mutually understood. For example, an educated person cannot deal effectively with an uneducated one because the latter would not understand the former's allusions. As shared experiences and attitudes are necessary for important social functions, similarity between persons is also important for those times when an individual feels a sentimental or nostalgic need to reminisce. Synchronisation of habits, temperament, desires and so on become significant when the situation is one where they both want to engage in some activity at the same time and in the same depth, such as studying, shopping, going out to the movies, or embarking on a journey. When a mutually beneficial activity can be performed alone, such as reading, gardening, cooking, or sewing, then one does not necessarily have to seek out companions with similar traits. Further, in order to balance the uncertain and chaotic interpersonal activities that are connected to career, many desire to have secure and predictable interactions in private life. Personality and experiential resemblances bring ease of social transaction which compensates for the dissatisfaction of dealing with people who are dissimilar to oneself in the workplace. Hence, there are relatively few restraints in situations where homology is present, such as in a relationship where the parties cohabit or otherwise spend large amounts of time together.

Just as individuals choose friends based on similarity in race, personality, background, attitudes, and behaviour, they choose an opposite-sex love interest using comparable criteria. However adequate one might find general similarity in a same-sex relationship, a deep friendship between the sexes requires extensive mutual support and compensation. Young people form associations in the attempt to find a 'mirror' for their attitudes and behaviour, without necessarily seeking to obtain something more deeply emotionally gratifying. Such a relationship is bound to be more self-centred, where people surround themselves with a panoply of interchangeable figures. Thus, what is important in a same-sex relationship might not be very important in a cross-sex friendship, and vice versa.

To these psychological factors are sometimes added ideas related to baser instincts. With human beings, there is an added psychological goal of a perpetuation of self, specifically by defining and maintaining one's own self-image. Consequently, out of awkwardness, and in striving to find common ground, young men often focus on the rudimentary or biological nature of male-female relations, conceptions which are tied to perpetuation of family and race. Everyone agrees that this is, after all, what 'mating' is ultimately about in the larger world of physical nature. The physical charms are accentuated, and a man finds some safety and relief in the romantic idea of the soft, warm embrace of a woman, which validates his manhood without threatening it.[2]

In the modern context, studies demonstrate that establishing a common ground between men and women indeed has a positive impact. The probability of an intimate opposite-sex relationship being deemed 'happy' is often increased if there is similitude in education and social class,[3] race,[4] and religion.[5] Homology in personality and status also produces greater equality in the performance of physical and emotional tasks, as well as a greater dependence and commitment, a lower level of conflict, and a higher level of satisfaction with the relationship.[6] Differences in personality traits and social background, on the other hand, might increase the risk of breakup.[7] Hence, close friendships between people are often not predicated on the coincidence of ideological positions and social policy questions; religious matters are important only when such ideas are endorsed and circulated by organised social movements. We can therefore see that 'trivial' habits and matters of taste are *highly* important.[8]

As the intimate friendship is not the only group to which a person can belong, men and women must view their relationship within the larger context of society. The concept of 'similarity' implies a sameness in social rank, so if two people are similar in many traits, then they must be approximately equal in social standing. Since Western society stresses career achievement and materialistic distinction, the similitude in a male-female relationship might clash with this rank advancement. However, there is evidence that individuals, in seeking a mate, focus more on attaining harmony in personality, than in achieving higher rank or prestige.[9] This is not to say rank and other social components have no value, but that rank has a lesser value in these relationships than in same-sex relationships. Indeed, often cross-sex associations are initiated because a man trying to 'score' with a girl, in order to raise his status by getting a girlfriend through daring behaviour, or rule-breaking. Nonetheless, we find that in the modern context, aspects of the close friendship are prioritised in the same way regardless of romantic involvement. In same-sex relationships, concordance in personality evidently comes first, then rank; in opposite-sex relationships, personality is also primary, but is followed more distantly by rank compared to same-sex relationships. Perhaps seeking stability and predictability, people go out of their way to choose mates who have similar traits, especially in regards to 'minor' aspects of temperament and disposition. They might use the relationship to improve their standing or rank in the group (as young people often do), but the test of relationship viability is level of agreement in feelings towards work, school, popular culture, clothes, food, etc.

Although it is natural for a person to desire to make friendships on the basis of similar traits, it is equally natural for that person to seek out people who can add to his or her knowledge, and compensate for weaknesses. Thus, it is possible that one can be strongly attracted to another, because the latter has traits that one does not have. One can be attracted to someone else because one sees a trait that one approves of, or admires. What is often admired is either a trait that one possesses, or a trait that one would like to possess, but does not.

Of course, it would be unreasonable for someone to be drawn to someone else if the other person presents subjectively unpleasant characteristics; however, it is understandable that one would desire the companionship of someone who is fundamentally different, if one believed that a mutual *enhancement* of life could take place within that relationship. Indeed, it would be unwise *not* to take advantage of this *complementarity*, which can lead to firmer, more resilient marriage, through a dovetailing and interweaving of interests and background. When someone is able to effectively draw upon the resources of another, only an improvement in the life situation can occur. The couple act as a coordinated unit, and every challenge strengthens the relationship, making it more and more difficult for them to separate. Therefore, the relationship is made whole and functional by different aspects; while deep mutual respect is the skeleton, and similarity of temperament, traits, and experiences that makes up the flesh, it is the dissimilarity is the muscle and sinew. Indeed, the couple no longer have a mere 'relationship', but have attained a true, deep bond, an inextricable connection with each other.

Similitude and divergence can have multifaceted effects on the relationship, but the impact is often not immediately apparent. Working under the assumption that the individual is as equally pleased to see a trait in himself as in other people, the list of admired traits that he desires in the perfect mate would be very similar to the one that he believes himself to possess. That being the case, we would expect that in relationship dyads, both individuals possess at least a few major traits in common. However, as differences between people can be quite beneficial, the recognition of dissimilarity in experience leads to the establishment of one's own unique domain of knowledge, which builds respect, and consequently a more open relationship, where independent thinking can be tolerated. On the other hand, dissimilarity can cause certain impediments, as one cannot really act to accomplish goals in areas one knows little about. Heterology tends to keep a critical distance between persons, and divergence of traits also inhibits assertiveness. Although many relationships are built on similarity in background and opinions, the lack of experience with complementary relationships does not usually have deleterious effects, as people have others readily at hand, often parents and relatives, to compensate for their weaknesses. Nonetheless, when it comes to relations with the other sex, they are out on their own, and then this lack of experience with heterology becomes a hindrance. An intimate relationship might function in a simple manner if there is only homology, and little use is made of positive differences. This type of relationship can bring certain limited rewards after some period of time.

We can see that the *conjunction of similarity and complementarity in background and temperament has an important role in fulfilling the personal ideal of love.* In order to reach the highest type of relationship, the *apotheosis*, then substantive personality similarities and differences must be accommodated intelligently and wisely by both members, as history has shown us that the attainment of any high goal requires the greatest diligence in gathering and utilising resources. Hence, to fulfill the desire for completeness in life requires forethought and planning. Nevertheless, when a person's mind does not operate in a sophisticated manner, that person devolves to using simple devices to get what he or she wants. Because the exigencies of modern life have banished higher-level thinking, depth and cooperation are relegated to a secondary status, and only a superficial agreement is perceived to be necessary in companionate relationships. If a person reckons, in a simplistic manner, that the only qualities that are 'positive' in another person are those qualities that are *similar to his own*, then any relationship with that other person would be far from the highest quality. Relationships, especially of a close variety, must involve a careful evaluation of the whole person, with all traits judged on their intrinsic merit. Using a narrow perspective in the search for a love interest, and only accepting someone who is substantively similar to oneself in temperament and background, means that the ideal of love has become *defective,* because it is satisfied with incomplete evaluations and limited interactions. Equality in attitudes and beliefs between two persons is good for a relationship, but without meaningful *complementing* differences, that relationship is weak and unbalanced and is destined to founder.

From the foregoing, we see that there are strong indications that homology, that is, similarity between two people, is extremely important at least in the *formative* or beginning stages of relationships, with heterology, and its positive resultant of complementarity, taking a secondary role. Since many people do not seem to understand what is necessary to attain ideal companionship, we must seek out and investigate first how men and women evaluate the other person's character, or to be more precise, the visible 'artefact' of their character, the collection of attributes that they reveal to the outside world, namely their personality.

Chapter 2

The Issue of Personality

*C*onsidering how well the evidence shows that similarity between partners can preserve individual independence, there should be little surprise about the finding that most marriages of the present day are strongly homologous.[10] Indeed, on attributes such as age, race, region of origin, education, attitudes, political and religious affiliation, matching is very high, on the order of 50% to 100%. Matching in cognitive abilities and psychiatric disorders is only about 20% to 50%. There is little evidence from these reports of negative correlations, wherein people seek dissimilarity more than similarity. Moreover, attributes do not appear to converge during marriage, but are there largely from the beginning.[11] The strong correlations in the larger areas of background are in keeping with our postulate that people will generally seek homology in their intimate relationships.

However, these studies also show that the matching of attributes which relate to 'personality' is low, usually below 20%. Why is there so little correlation between spouses in the area called 'personality'? One reason might be that people first use 'plain facts' about individuals as the basis for judging whether a relationship should proceed. This would include factors of age, race, education and so on. For the relationship to blossom, there must be some constructive differences in personality, whilst other areas of personality are desired to be similar, thus resulting in an absence of high correlation. The mixing of similarity and complementarity in personality would largely nullify correlations, indicating that homology is important for larger factors, but not for many individual specific traits. Another reason might be that 'personality' is difficult to quantify, and an estimation of it might not substantively contain all the traits that are relevant to a companionate relationship, such as minor habits, everyday decision-making, and ideology.

We also note that temperament *per se* is often not incorporated into personality assessments, so couples who are similar in temperament might not betray much similarity in 'personality', as defined by sociology. Research demonstrates that much, if not most, of *temperament* (introversion, extroversion, work, and leisure habits) is genetically derived. To be clear, we are not saying that most personality traits are genetically influenced, but only one area, that of temperament. Therefore, two members of the same ethnic group are likely to be more similar to each other in genetic material, and also in temperament, compared to two people belonging to different groups. Although members of the same ethnic group might have similar temperaments, which might produce similar habits and thinking patterns, it is the *interaction* of innate traits with social entities and affiliations that determines what type of personality is eventually manifested.

If it were true that genetics was largely responsible for all fundamental innate divergences in personality, encompassing intellect, emotions, as well as temperament, then it would become quite difficult to create a good match. If most men and women were servants to many different inalterable instincts, arranging a homologous union would indeed be frustratingly arduous. The ordinary expectation would then be of a 'romantic relationship' streaked with discord and enmity. We do not, however, have any evidence that genetics plays such an important role in personality formation, and indeed, there is much research which betrays an inability to convincingly connect thinking patterns with biology.

There is reason to believe that *differences* in temperament might exist between the sexes, which are not only an essential element in the deeper attraction between the sexes, but also function to create a mutual *improvement* of personality, character, and lifestyle. Without doubt, differences in personality can produce friction, yet the attraction to someone unlike ourselves makes sense, if one acknowledges that there is an almost indomitable fascination with things unknown, due, at the very least, to the *strong innate human propensity to learn.* Nevertheless, it is more than simple curiosity that produces a truly complex and intense fascination with another person. There has to be an understanding at some level of consciousness that transformation is possible. Since such unions can and do occur, the belief that major trait differences are counterproductive is largely incorrect.

Thus, similarity and homology might be what people are comfortable with, but complementarity is what they ultimately seek in order for true love to come alive. It cannot be overemphasised, however, that *although the founding and continuing vitality of a relationship is often expedited through homology, a deeply rewarding relationship can only be attained through the crucial presence of positive heterology.* The most successful way in which homology and heterology can enhance a relationship is through joint learning as a central experience. Whether the learning occurs due to individual interest or due to external necessity, it provides the couple with critical information about each other's strengths and weaknesses, information that acts to build respect. Further, both add important shared experiences to their lives that increase the level of similarity between each another, accordingly increasing mutual attractiveness. Most importantly, where weaknesses are revealed, and difficulties threaten successful completion of a project, another can use their strengths to step in to 'save the day', which also increases desirability and respect.

For people seeking a marriage partner, there is a range of traits which can potentially be used for comparison. Age, academic qualifications, employment status, income, ethnic group affiliation, hobbies, previous dating relationships, social activity—all are pieces of information that go into the 'portrait' that becomes the character. However, equal in importance to the qualitative value of these data is the sequence in which they are obtained. The *first* critical appraisal by the couple is often not of each other's background, but of each other's *opinions*. This is reasonable, because in Western cultures it is easier for acquaintances to enquire about each other's opinions, than to pose questions that delve into the details of their respective backgrounds; the latter might be seen as 'intrusive'. Furthermore, since opinions concern not only the past and present status of a person, but their future status as well, they are actually more important than most other attributes.

Many people will want even greater depth, and will explore another person's *beliefs*, those more strongly felt judgments and appraisals. Hence, beliefs on the rules govern the relationship itself would be particularly appropriate, since without congruence here, the relationship might easily falter. This is especially important since intimate relationships have more rules that facilitate close-ness, and cover social and emotional factors, than non-intimate relationships, where the rules used are primarily for maintaining distance.[12] The couple would have to agree not only on attitudes concerning abstract and practical matters, but also on the rules that would govern their own friendship. 'Truth in disclosure' not only makes for steadier and deeper relationships, it is also a critical component in the character of the virtuous person. However, it might not be possible to fully determine the facts until one is well into a relationship, and so one is exposed to some significant risk of loss.

From the foregoing, it can be seen that agreement on certain issues is highly important in setting the *pace of interactions during courtship*. Initial evaluations of another person during the pre-dating or early dating stages are limited to a general consideration of characteristics such as race, religion, appearance, and previous marital status. Because of the large number of candidates available in modern industrialised societies, the mental and physical re-sources made available for such an evaluation must be considerably limited if all candidates are to be dealt with equally and fairly. The belief is that if one matches both in theory and in practise opinions on these areas, there is greater likelihood that there will be congru-ity in other, more detailed questions. When well-educated people have a stronger convergence in these areas, they are more likely to be well-matched. The result if that being in a social environment of a campus or classroom is more likely to yield a quick easy 'yes' to a date enquiry. Random encounters on a college campus, in a dormitory, classroom or social function, often carry a good chance of turning into friendships, because it is likely that people will have the same opinions about a number of important issues, such as their personal outlook on married life and on dating a member of another social group.

However, different phases in the relationship bring different kinds of questions, and different kinds of answers. When a man and woman first meet, they attempt to discern each other's position on important issues pertaining to a potential relationship. If general opinions on an issue do not have much clustering, then there will be many encounters that end fruitlessly, bringing a certain sense of frustration. If a time limit is imposed, then people will go through a number of such encounters, and settle on the best although not ideal person; there is a greater likelihood of opinion incongruity and thus greater friction in the relationship. If no time limit is imposed, then the groups that are more variable in opinion will take longer to find the right person, compared to those who have opinion clustering. In the latter scenario, the 'goodness of fit' of a relationship originating in a low-variability (homogenous) group versus a high-variability (heterogenous, diverse) group will not be very different, if random chance appertains in all cases. Given time, most people will find a compatible spouse, with similar characteristics, regardless of whether the members of their group are generally similar or not similar to each other. To the extent that social forces influence personal plans, 'deadline' pressures can be implicated as a reason for bad marriages in diverse societies.

Hence, there must be a delineation between the first stage, where simple procedures are used to see if the couple can get along at all, and later stages, where complex and sometimes protracted methods reveal the filigree work of personality. The congruence of ideas about the 'goodness' of the relationship itself only validates its existence, allowing it to move forward, but does not actually bring the couple any *closer* together, as only true homology in temperament, attitudes, opinions, and behaviour can do that. It is an intriguing aspect of human affair that major differences in culture and family background become quickly apparent in a relationship that is mixed in fundamental views, perhaps eclipsing an initial rosy assessment that was based only on an evaluation of beliefs of a general nature. Even though it is important at all stages to reassure oneself that a cognitive alliance exists in the major arenas of life, certainty is all the more critical in later stages if emotional consummation is to be achieved.

After dating over a period of time, and after the relationship has deepened to an extent, the couple invariably believe they have learned more about one another than what would be known in a casual friendship. Although not yet married, the couple do experience many parallel situations to that of a married couple; hence, possible friction might still arise over differences in opinion, for example, about the roles of men and women in married life. However, because there is already some investment of resources in the relationship, the likelihood of a breakup might be less than expected. It is only after marriage, when abstract issues and questions become quite concrete, that serious disagreement is likely to arise. If agreement on issues is forced, and ideas are not clearly and genuinely expressed during courtship, then married life can be a disappointment. In fact, it becomes inauthentic and false.

Clearly, the expectation that men and women, in an intimate relationship, will agree on all areas is not realistic. However, we have seen that the timing, the extent, and category of agreement and disagreement all have major ramifications on the formation and maintenance of the relationship, and it would be advantageous for us to identify *which factors most strongly influence opinion and in what directions*. We have seen in other works (Sporer 2010A, 2010B) that one area is commonly found in the formation of friendships, careers, personal habits, status, and social rank, namely that of *education*. As education would logically be expected to exert an influence on thinking, and as education is a critical part of the modern life course, the amount of institutional instruction might be associated with the direction and strength of general opinions. Further, if it is true that education can affect opinions, with differing results for men and for women, the methods of fulfilling the modern cultural desire of matching 'like for like' in marriage, of creating 'equality' in married life, are much more subservient to individual factors. In this case, a man or woman's personality would not be the dull product of biology, but potentially a rich tapestry of divergent experiences and thinking patterns, from which a spouse could well learn and benefit.

Chapter 3

Opinions About Us

*A*ccordingly, let us now examine in greater detail the effect that education has on the direction and strength of opinions. It is beyond debate that the more college education one has, the more theories one is offered, and the more information one assimilates. The institutions of higher education often use materials that draw from the same sources, the same authorities, and thus already there is a similarity in the ideas that are taught in the classroom. From the instructor's perspective, there are 'standard' concepts that are taught especially in the basic courses, and these have conceptual congruence across the different courses on a campus, as well as across different institutions of learning. Students are therefore exposed to a consistent flow of information, which they internalise and utilise as the basis for their opinions. Well-educated persons have been exposed to a wealth of putatively factual knowledge and theories, which, however, often contradict one another, making it difficult to hold convincing opinions with absolute certainty. College also encourages dissent and novelty, so individuals are likely to form their own theories, in some cases not because they really find it necessary, but because they simply wish to appear 'academic'. All of this means that the imprint that the educational system makes on students will remain for years afterwards.

Within the college environment are mechanisms which have the ability to alter opinions, in the sense that they can move the views of different persons into conformity, so that they can state that they 'for', 'against' something, or alternatively, state they are 'not sure' or have 'no opinion'. Further, experiences with prioritising and sorting data and constructing hierarchies of information, make well-educated individuals more comfortable with spreading out responses along an attitudinal spectrum. On an opinion scale of say 1 to 7, with 1 being very much in favour of something, and 7 being very much against it, middling, equivocal, or 'weak' values (3, 4, or 5) are not uncommon. The confluence of these factors results sometimes in an alteration in beliefs. Indeed, it is not unusual that long-held and strong convictions, whilst not rejected, are significantly reduced in intensity. What might start out as a belief on one end of the scale, say at 7, might at some point settle somewhere in the middle, such as on 4. Diversity, although making debate between friends and/or colleagues spirited and interesting, can produce acrimonious arguments between husband and wife. Accordingly, if education does indeed have the impact on opinions that we postulate it to have, it would be of interest to discover the specific dynamics involved.

The most important issues a couple would confront would be those relating to the *relationship itself* and the people involved. We therefore present a selection of questions relating to those issues, asked in a survey of unmarried, non-cohabiting people under the age of 35.[13] We find clear evidence of patterns in the strength and direction of opinions, and we summarise the results in the following table:

TABLE 1. RANGES OF OPINIONS ON MARRIED LIFE

QUESTIONS (paraphrased)	CHANGE IN DIVERSITY OF OPINIONS (as education increases)		CHANGE IN AVG OPINION (due to increased education)
	MALE	FEMALE	
Would you like to get married? (A3-2.)	Moderately diverse to moderately strongly singular	As for males	From 'agree' to 'strongly agree'
Is it better for a person to marry than to be single? (A3-3.)	Moderately singular, little change	Moderately singular to moderately diverse	From 'agree' to 'neither'
How would life be different now if married, in terms of personal freedom? (A3-6.)	Moderately diverse to strongly singular	Moderately diverse to moderately singular	From 'same' to 'somewhat worse'
. . . in terms of friendship with others? (A3-8.)	Singular, little change	Moderately singular to strongly singular	From 'somewhat better' to 'same'
. . . in terms of relations with parents? (A3-9.)	Same as above	Same as above	Same as above
How important is saving money before marriage? (A4-1.)	Strong singularity to great diversity	As for males	From very important to centre; outlier at 'not at all important' for females
How important is it for you to have a job? (A4-2.)	As above	As above	As above

QUESTIONS (paraphrased)	CHANGE IN DIVERSITY OF OPINIONS (as education *increases*)		CHANGE IN AVG OPINION (due to *increased* education)
	MALE	FEMALE	
How important is it for you for your partner to have a job? (A4-3.)	As above	As above	As above
How important is it for you to finish your education? (A4-4.)	Moderately singular to moderately diverse	As above	As above
How important is it for your partner to his/her education? (A4-5.)	Moderately singular to great diversity	As above	As above
Would you marry someone who has been married before? (A4-8.)	Moderately diverse to moderately singular	Moderately diverse to moderately singular	Males: from about centre to moderately unwilling; Females: remaining at about centre
Would you marry someone with children? (A4-9.)	Diverse to moderately singular	Diverse to moderately singular	Males: Moderately willing to moderately unwilling; Females: generally not willing to not at all willing
Would you marry someone who earned much more than you? (A4-12.)	Moderately diverse, little change	Moderately high singularity to moderately high diversity	Males: moderately willing; Females: very willing to moderately willing

QUESTIONS (paraphrased)	CHANGE IN DIVERSITY OF OPINIONS (as education *increases*)		CHANGE IN AVG OPINION (due to *increased* education)
	MALE	FEMALE	
Would you marry someone of a different race? (A4-16.)	Moderately diverse to moderately singular	As for males	From moderately not willing to quite unwilling
Would you marry someone who was not good looking? (A4-17.)	Greatly diverse to strongly singular	As for males	Males: centre to moderately not willing; Females: centre to moderately strong centre

The first two questions in this table have the following possible replies: Strongly agree, agree, neither, disagree, strongly disagree, and refused/no answer.

The next three questions have the following possible responses: Much worse, somewhat worse, same, somewhat better, much better, refused/no answer/don't know.

The remaining questions have responses placed on a scale of 1 to 7, with not at all willing (or important) at 1, and very willing (or important) at 7, with an additional response of no answer/refused/don't know.

Source: Chadwick & Heaton (1992), pp 22–47.

We see from the preceding table, that *higher* education *reduces diversity of opinion* concerning issues of a general, cursory nature that might be relevant largely *before* serious dating (courtship) begins: Whether one oneself should marry (strongly agree); whether one's relations with friends and parents after marriage are improved (remain the same); whether one should marry someone who is physically unattractive (centre, no clear opinion); whether one should marry someone of a different race (not willing); whether one should marry someone with children (not willing).

In regards to the first issue, whether one onself should marry, let us dispel a misconception, that it is incongruous for educated people to stress the importance of marriage, because such persons find they can engage in a wider range of pursuits that can offer a *suitable alternative to marriage*. While it is true that college educated people use their academic achievement, and the higher income that usually results form it, to pursue many activities, career related and personal, it is clear that such activities do not supplant the accomplishments of married life. This underlines the continuing preeminence of *companionship* over autonomy in modern life. In any case, in the areas cited above, well-educated couples reach more agreement, and thus would tend to have a more harmonious dating relationship.

Whilst we might reasonably assume that a correspondence in opinion would be parallelled by correspondence with other background attributes, education is evidently exceptional in that similar school experience does *not* necessarily mean similar opinions in all areas. We find in our table that greater education brings *more diversity in issues* that are more substantive, specific, and that become important *once the marriage is underway*, in the following areas: Whether finishing an education, having savings, and having a job, are important in married life; whether husbands should earn more than wives; whether someone should marry in general (for oneself and others); whether marriage increases freedom. Increased heterology in opinion arises because of a *confusion between separating roles*, such as wife and career woman. A woman with high education credentials, it is believed, *should* live out her potential by earning a good deal of money, but at the same time she should *not* compete with her husband. Perhaps the higher earnings engendered by advanced formal schooling makes people less concerned about economic issues, because education gives them freedom in a career. This reveals an interesting potential area of conflict between independence and marriage, where a wife's dedication to home life is devalued by the belief that the freedom 'bought' by education must be exercised. There need be no conflict as long as the individual understands that the primary role of education is intellectual, not physical, emancipation.

Thus, the higher the education of either men or women, the more *diverse* their opinions become in certain areas. Although a man and woman's experiences of obtaining higher education might be similar, and accordingly draw them together, that very education might have created a divergence of opinion that makes concurrence difficult on other issues.

We should also understand that in many cases people have views that are not delineated or differentiated, but could be placed in the 'not sure or 'don't know' part of the spectrum. Two people might say that they have 'similar' opinions even when both say they are 'not sure' about whether to agree or disagree with principle. From the evidence presented, it is apparent that the better educated often tend to be somewhere in the middle values on an opinion scale, but less educated people are often intolerant of ambiguity, of 'grey areas', and tend to cluster at the extremes. However, educational experience might also create greater similarity in opinions in other areas, so making it difficult to offer any easy explanation for this phenomenon.

We can see that the latter questions cited above, concerning earnings and employment, are especially important, *as it appears that divergence does not bring heterophily, that is, a pleasure in significant interpersonal differences*. No constructive compensation is found in these kinds of differences; instead, they cause challenges to status and to the concept of equality. Evidence for this unhappiness is found in the observation that highly paid college-educated women find marital dissolution a considerably more probable occurrence than their lower-paid educational cohort.[14] This is partly the result of a *reification* of potentially contentious issues, that is, making an abstract concept into a material reality; these issues include whether a husband should earn more than his wife, whether he should be fully employed, and whether marriage significantly decreases personal freedom; significant divergence from parity produces the feeling that mutual respect no longer exists.[15] For those wives who do not work or who have a low-paying part-time job, their divorce potential is much lower than their well-educated counterparts, because attitudes about a husband's relative earning power are never treated as anything more than mere conjecture. There is no true formula that can be utilised, since the wife and husband do not engage in similar work roles. If the wife attempted to make a comparison in relative earning power, the husband would say she is 'comparing apples to oranges'.

These processes that affect that similarity or diversity of opinions produce alterations to courtship. If within a particular environment there is *less* variability (i.e. more similarity) on opinions, there is usually a greater chance of a favourable union for two people if they meet by simple random chance, as the odds are increased that they will have the same opinion on an issue. For example, if two people, sitting side-by-side in the campus cafeteria, begin to discuss marriage, then there will be a fairly high likelihood that they will both state the preference that they themselves wish to marry, as the majority of people on that campus hold these very beliefs. Obviously, the dating process is facilitated in this case.

We should realise that not only does being in the majority help people finding others with similar thinking, but also being in the *minority*. When dissimilarity is high, the chance of a match is actually increased as well. This less-than-obvious factor further illustrates the dangers of forced similarity. When there is clustering of opinions around one point of the scale, then there is a clear majority group and clear minority group. The member of the minority will become disenchanted with the views of the majority, and will seek others who believe what they do. At social functions of a specialised or idiosyncratic variety, two such 'outsiders' standing side-by-side might make conversation and possible friendship. The stronger the outsider status, the more likely they would be to actively seek others of similar beliefs, increasing the odds of making a match. Randomness is being circumvented because people are assiduously looking to connect with others of the same type of thinking. Thus, if one is indifferent to marriage, and the majority are strongly in favour of it, then one might associate with those who are similarly indifferent. 'Indifference' does not mean absolute refusal, so it is possible that an individual with a weak desire for emotional gratification might marry anyway for material or status purposes. It might precisely be this minority association that makes it *more* likely that both spouses are indifferent to marriage, since they were more likely to fraternise with each other, than with people who strongly believe in matrimony.[16] This situation is most likely to occur when the persons holding dissimilar beliefs are clearly different from most other people within a particular social context.

It is in the area of race that this effect is most socially obvious and most potentially divisive. One could initially believe that since college educated individuals generally are not willing to marry someone from another race (see Table I above), that these types of couples would be more poorly educated than average. However, it would appear that both husbands and wives in mixed marriages (black male-white female, white male-black female) tend to be significantly *better* educated, than black-black or white-white marriages. White men and women in college who tend to believe in the fundamental propriety of mixed-race relations and marriages would actively seek others who have the same attitudes. As racial minority groups in society are likely to accept such mixing, usually out of necessity, these would be more likely to meet, socialise, and possibly marry the whites they meet at 'idiosyncratic' or 'underground' gatherings. The effect is similar to that experienced by people who leave home in order to find love and support. Where a person, in one case, might go from one household to another, in this case, a person might go from one peer group or social group to another.

Even when there are similarities in certain basic beliefs, and a

relative ease of courtship, the black male-white female marriage
is evidently a stormy match, as it is much shorter in duration than
same race marriages; marital duration is on average similar between white male-black female and same-race marriage couples.[17]
The fact that there is *initial* agreement on issues does not guarantee
marital *longevity*, a point we make elsewhere and that cannot be
overemphasised. People might be very happy that they have met
someone who shares their views, possibly after a long period of
searching. The relationship might blossom into a good friendship,
but might not grow into a deep affectionate bond if a full dovetailing of characteristics is not made.

However, although they must deal with cultural clashes that are
as apparently unique to their relationship as a black male-white
female pair, white male-black female relationships seem to have
less divorce than other mixed-race marriages. White male-black
female marriages might endure longer than black male-white female marriages, because in the latter case, the couple are disadvan-
taged in *three* significant respects. One, their opinions are in the
minority for their educational group; two, their marriage is of a
minority type for their education group, and in general; three, the
head of household is a member of a minority race, resulting in an
unusual type of household structure. The last factor might make
the marriage untenable, because it is beyond the conceptions of
most people, that is, it is 'too deviant', beyond the fringe, by majority standards. *Even if the couple agrees on major issues, these other
divergences from social norms make it difficult for them to feel as if
they fit into society.* If the head of the household is a white man
married to a black woman, then the couple are deviant in only *two*
respects, making them more acceptable, as they have only two

'strikes' against them but not a third, allowing a greater degree of social integration. Further, if there is some basic acceptance into society, the relationship might be made *more* tolerable perhaps, because longer exposure to the educational system assists in the development of intellectual mechanisms and reasoned thinking that can defuse potential conflict. There is consequently a paradox: Although there is apparent equality in the relationship, even in mixed-race marriages, this equality is not matched by the relationship itself being equal to other relationships.

Thus, the over-demand for similarity might create unions that leave individuals poorly matched as spouses, and situated as social outsiders. The initial attraction between two college-educated people was the characteristic that they had a more open and liberal (non-conventional) attitude towards friendships. This attraction may have been reinforced by their similar attitudes about other issues due to their college education. However, challenging the relationship is not only a fundamental lack of agreement in important areas relating to married life, but an absence of complementarity. Further, there is a struggle with social exclusion, a fate that the demand for similarity was supposed to avoid. The principle we have been discussing, of minority groups distinguishing themselves from majority groups, would probably apply to other areas as well, but without the added factor of having to go outside one's own racial group. For example, the same effect applies to other areas where there is a division in belief, such as on the issue of physical appearance or marrying someone who has been married before. It is also possible that a higher than expected proportion of people who married divorced individuals with children are college graduates. Even though those with higher education evince the belief that it is wrong marrying someone who already has children, the fact that colleges offer venues for those who deviate from this norm might actually facilitate such unions.

In certain cases, people do consciously seek out others with very different opinions. We cite here one type of situation, that of the joining together of educated men and less educated women, resulting in the creation of a 'mixed' couple. Tired of what they see as the pusillanimous, 'wishy-washy', and even disloyal attitudes of educated women, intellectual men might be attracted to lesser-educated women, who possess strong and therefore stable ideas about work, savings, a husband's position in the household. One seeks uniformity of opinions, and one more often than not finds them in the lower classes. Hence, those men who spend their time in education developing their intellect, and thus putting off marriage, have a tendency to form heterologous unions, such as marrying well beneath their social class.

Two examples of this phenomenon drawn from history can be adduced. Rousseau and Descartes, both intelligent men who encouraged refinement and sophistication, took ordinary and probably illiterate servant girls as 'unofficial' wives. We know that Rousseau, much-attacked in his lifetime, saw loyalty as the main virtue of his mistress, whom he would eventually wed when he was 56. In contrast to their intellectual side, the emotional side of such men is poorly controlled and developed. Managing anger and frustration become very difficult and a simple woman that possesses a 'strong' personality and open nature helps to rebuild a damaged ego. They might even seek the 'archaic' or 'dangerous' woman—earthy, naïve and uncomplicated.[18] As higher education has become quite common in the Western world, the man of intellectual bent, staggered by the emotionally restrained and uncertain opinions of uneducated women, is by no means difficult to find, and this type of relationship is also hardly unusual.

We have seen in this chapter that opinions are indeed altered through the process of education, particularly higher or tertiary level education. After exposure to this tutelary environment, convergence of opinions is likely to occur on issues pertaining to whether one should marry, the type of person one should marry, and the type of background of that person. However, the same environment inspires diversity in opinions pertaining to the importance of savings, work experience, and education. Those materialistic 'nitty-gritty' areas of married life are evidently more susceptible to personal interpretation.

There is little doubt that men and women seek out members of the opposite sex who have similar opinions about basic issues, and often make such agreement a high priority. Certain institutions appear to have been given the task of making such agreement easier to find inside of the usual areas where men and women are likely to fraternise. However, divergence on issues will always exist to some extent, and the lack of coordination of views might create increasing friction over time, especially during the course of the marital relationship. There must be ways to reduce both the level of disagreement between spouses, and the level of negative reaction to whatever remaining divergence exists.

Chapter 4

Preserving Harmony

*A*greement on basic issues is always of import in all phases
of the relationship, and education evidently plays an important role
in forming or affecting such opinions. We should reiterate, however, that the most contentious issues that a couple can face are
actually *not related to issues of background or ethnicity*, since many
minor disagreements over opinions will cause a falling-out long
before these deeper issues become relevant. If there is little agreement in the early phase of dating or courtship due to divergent
opinions, the relationship will end; if there is good general agreement, then the relationship will proceed, but agreement on more
specific and more important issues, as we have been discussing,
will have to be achieved if the relationship is to be mutually
beneficial, harmonious and genuine. Behaviour, or a tendency to
a behaviour, as embodied in personality and temperament, is never
merely theoretical but are always concrete, and so it appears as a
'deeper' issue. However, whether an opinion is minor or major
depends on its pertinence to some aspect of life, either now or in
the future. An opinion about an issue that does not presently touch
the lives of the couple is considered 'abstract', but it can suddenly
turn 'concrete' if the issue must actually be acted upon.

This change in relevance can be seen in particular where a wife's

working full-time outside the home produces a number of potentially divisive issues: The issue of a wife making more than a husband, the issue of a wife's loss of freedom, the issue of a husband
being out of work, and the issue of a wife launching a supportive
role. In cases where the wife does not work, and/or a husband is
comfortably employed and well-paid, controversial but theoretical
points of view can lay dormant. Suddenly, this issue can become
concrete, and the opinion is no longer minor; as a result, the harmony of the relationship is threatened.[19] We can all agree that virtue is most numinous and spiritually compelling in stories of chival-
rous men who rescue chaste women in heroic combat, but the more
common scenario in which virtue is confronted might be of the
average man 'heroically' trying to pay the bills and support his wife
and family. So ironically, a fall from grace occurs not because the
knight could not bring himself to slay the dragon, but because a
husband could not agree with his 'damsel' about the *mundane*
aspects of life.

The greater diversity in opinions found among lesser-educated
individuals about issues relating to attractiveness, marriage goals,
children, race, and friends, is to a large extent a part of the Industrial Age's overall regrettable 'confusion' of values. As shall be seen
later on, the effects of migration, occupation, and loss of traditional
values have instigated such variability amongst local cultures that
it is difficult to state what, for example, a 'typical American' believes. Education is a homogenising influence which makes one
individual's opinions more similar to that of another, creating a
'levelling action' in dating and marital relationships. However,
education also creates new differences in opinion, which somewhat
reduce its benefits. Schooling is, therefore, highly useful to society

in cultivating productive citizens, but its shortcomings must be redressed by complex social adjustments. With or without higher education, people must resort to other, questionable methods to assure similarity in attitudes and behaviour between partners.

The modern world's demand for material well-being and a high standard-of-living has resulted in the necessity of the educated citizen. Yet this materialism has also created *unbalanced* societies largely due to migration and loss of direction from customary practises. Such imbalances create diversity of opinions and attitudes. *Education brings homogeneity back to opinions, thus restoring, to a certain extent, a balance in relationships.* But it should be remembered that even though two people are reconciled to each other, sometimes through difficult circumstances if they are outside the mainstream in some way, that this does not guarantee relationship viability, as the very fact that the struggle took place due to their minority status, might create problems with larger society. As we have seen, this affects people marrying others of different races and backgrounds, a problem in populations containing diverse cultures. More importantly, when similarity is the main focus, and not cooperation, then finding someone who is similar will increase their worth, but other areas that need to be discussed, including ethnicity and background, are ignored as value areas. This reticence, unfortunately, cannot last forever as the press of external challenges come upon the 'well-matched' couple. The crucial match, as we shall see, is not necessarily in opinions or traits, but in the willingness to change and accommodate.

Previous generations dealt in different and astute ways with the issue of psychological matching in order to preserve marital harmony. When did Western society begin to develop difficulties in dealing with interpersonal differences? Using various demographic, cultural, and economic indicators of social change, the transitional period between 'traditional' and 'modern' can reasonably be centred at about 1800. Hence, principles of relationship arose from a multiplicity of factors that operated at a level very close to the individual. Although there was homogeneity of culture within this circle of villages, perfect similarity was lacking, and major dissimilarities were not at all unusual. Further, there was no attempt to increase similarity, as the spouse accepted the characteristics that they brought into the marriage as issues that could be handled effectively. The small village, a prototype of the past, contained few choices of marriage partner, and on many occasions people would out of necessity choose a spouse not very similar to themselves in personality, background, or temperament. Sometimes, family history about the great-grandparent who married a girl 'outside the community' reveals differences so exaggerated as to challenge modern sensibilities. Were people simply indolent, and accepted the divergences between husband and wife? Not likely, since people in Western societies often measured the success of any relationship by its closeness. And closeness was based on how much one would be willing to exclude from one's life for the sake of the other. Since married couples were presumed to have the closest of friendships, then all other things became secondary.

The material or financial set-up, however, of the household is the next most important factor for a happy marriage. Once finances had stabilised, the couple would learn how to live with each other, and this ability was believed to be a nearly universal natural talent. Indeed, strife usually occurred when money was inadequate; as long as the basic physical needs were met, the emotional side would inevitably take care of itself. This, however, presupposes that the couple had subordinated their responsibilities to other people, in order to put themselves in the right frame of mind for this mutual transformation to take place. The process was private but usually affected by the experiences and beliefs of others in the community. Culture, however, the accumulated wisdom of many generations, provides many elements of normative thinking. Accordingly, the customary mores of a parish, hamlet, village or some larger community, might have induced, influenced or reinforced the idea at all social levels that *entrustment* between two people was paramount for a successful marriage.

In spite of the force of circumstances reducing the range of potential marriage partners, society saw married life as not exceedingly difficult for a number of reasons that we can deduce from our knowledge of relationships and history. Firstly, in order to obtain an orderly family and household, people were willing to *compromise,* which not seen as a personal defeat or admission of weakness. Secondly, in the less demanding societies of the past, people could be more *pliant* and *flexible* than today, readily altering their activities to accommodate the needs of others in the family. Thirdly, people had belief systems that were located within a *narrower spectrum*, thus making it unlikely that the individual would be called upon to make extensive changes. Fourthly, as people *grow more similar* to each other as they get older, then people could marry others who are mostly similar, but also quite different from themselves in certain respects; there was basically no need to over-stress homology. There was also no need for a lengthy 'preparation' for married life, as circumstances in marriage did not have to be radically different from that found in single life. One could marry someone significantly older or younger than oneself without worrying very much about compatibility.

In this scenario, a strong attitude of independence would admittedly be difficult to negotiate, and the essentially private strategy described above was modified by the forces of the Industrial Revolution. One could say that the hallmark of the modern period is an almost constant shifting of plans. With reference to the labour demands of factory automation, early in the modern period inflexibility and uncooperativeness were established as social norms. Most private strategies, of whatever kind, were often delayed or obviated. The economy did not tolerate much individual creativity on the job, nor did it allow much choice of occupation. In addition, in the fear of losing their identity, people became more nationalist, class-orientated, and group-orientated, making their beliefs more narrow and even less amenable to change. The tactic of seeking the protection of the group arose from migration, which caused people to inhabit new areas where ideas and patterns of behaviour were different from the ones they knew so well. Words that avow conformity to larger aims, and thus assure survival of the group, have become more important than personal goals and virtuous *actions*. Before a person was ultimately respected for how he handled his personal affairs, through honesty and integrity; now, identity is bound up with what a person's *opinions*. We should stress that opinions are not synonymous with beliefs; opinions can change and are often obtained from social trends. Hence, virtue declined and simplistic notions became ingrained in people's minds.

The ultimate goal of marriage, to achieve affection and support, has in no way changed, and our European ancestors understood that this harmony was achieved through compromise, flexibility, and accommodation, items that made up the various cultural 'formulas' for married life. However, the *methods* used in the attempt to achieve this great goal of harmony have steadily been revised over the past 150 years, often with poor results. Some might rephrase this, and say that the *ideal* of marriage has changed, but this would be misleading if one were only to think of an ideal as the end result of a series of actions, and not the actions and the result together as a whole. It should be clear that one cannot exist without the other, and so when we speak of the ideal, we speak of both deeds and outcome. More accurately we should say that the *traditional ideal* is no longer pursued. Most people still possess an ideal of a love where traditional methods lead to a positive outcome, but these older methods are no longer considered viable, and so a positive result in marriage is in doubt. This does not mean that the traditional ideal has been abandoned; indeed, most people still keep it in mind, although it may have been 'put on hold'.

More likely, a new 'ideal' has replaced the old ideal. If one person refuses to marry because of objections about another person's attitudes or behaviour, then this is a case of individual devaluation; but if the suspicion is of married life *in general*, regardless of who is the spouse, then it might be part of a worldview where people globally are devalued. This is not something that can come about unless major changes in thinking have occurred. In our day, the talk about goals in marriage have become more common, as people many fail to attain even a modicum of success in their personal relations. It is precisely when marriages are *not* succeeding that the 'ideal' is thought about all the more passionately, and debated all the more loudly, albeit through symbols and metaphors. However, this 'ideal' that is being discussed is often defective.

In reality, from earliest times human beings have held a strong personal belief in a particular kind of *exemplary relationship*. Whether the individual reached it or not, the model of life that was seen as most appropriate persisted and endured. The people of the past did not analyse themselves and each other incessantly, nor did worry about attaining an *externally*-derived paragon of relationship; but that does not mean that they did not create, using their own means, such a paradigm of excellence. Throughout life they could have quietly carried a model of the 'perfect family' that would be fitting for them, their spouses, and their children.

Consequently, the changes in *conceptualisation* of traditional history and culture have made a difference in the ways the ideal marriage is viewed. Over the last four generations, it is perhaps the inordinate shift in the basic components of marriage, and indeed in all of society, that has made people in the Western world forget about their collective origins. The people of the past have become temporal foreigners to many, in relation to which one can put oneself in whatever fantasy or escapist orientation one wishes. Concepts different from the present time that challenge ideals can be discarded without much guilt. Probably the one fantasy most highly regarded is about noble modern man valorously struggling to reach a humanitarian 'ideal', outshining the depravity of his dull-witted peasant forbear who cared for nothing except satisfying the cravings of his belly and his loins.[20] This portrayal is often encountered in the popular media, reinforcing the 'great' set of concepts relating to married life.

If the old ideal of love has not been surrendered, and people have become more selfish and less accommodative, what marital strategy has supplanted the traditional one?

We can say that the modern marital strategy hinges, to a large extent, on a *new definition of dependence*. European cultures have always accepted the idea the women and men from an early age can be dependent, emotionally and materially, on other people, and still retain their individuality. Indeed, enjoying beneficial support from others in the pursuit of attaining one's life goals has always been considered not only appropriate, but essential. However, under certain circumstances, where a person's actions are based on self-centred motivations, this reliance on others can become problematic because the boundaries of appropriate behaviour are not respected. *Thus, it is from this selfishness and over-dependence on others that a preoccupation with similarity has arisen.* We can reduce these elements to this formula:

+ *Self-centeredness*
+ *Emotional Over-dependance*
− *Constructive Cooperation*

= *Excessive Demand for Similarity*

Let us now elaborate on the origin and maintenance of the factors listed above.

Firstly, in regard to *self-centeredness,* the demands of modern society often encourage people to partake of a resource without giving due compensation. The phenomenon of increased stress in the workplace, and increased dissonance with, and distance from, other family members, have produced a serious isolation of the individual in many Western societies. Such a person might feel that his own family has demonstrated a lack of substantive interest in the affairs of his life, and therefore, as compensation, he tries to obtain emotional support from a spouse, but without giving any in return. The relationship carries only a false impression of harmony, an immature lack of compassion that has been carried over from childhood into a poorly developed but artful adult mentality. In the past, where European culture stressed the superiority of adult prestige and respect over the helplessness and inadequacy of childhood, men and women were more secure in believing in themselves, and would then work harder to yield time, attention, and other resources, without feeling threatened; whatever interpersonal differences that existed would have been reduced or disappeared over time. Hence, for the people of the past, it was not as important that they should be greatly compatible from the beginning.

Secondly, the great improvement in economic conditions has been responsible for the *decline of constructive dependence on, and assistance from, others*. Material aspects can now be adjusted and modified, making them more amenable to the individual's control. For example, sewing and knitting (traditionally in the wife's domain) are now carried out by professional firms, and repairs and maintenance (traditionally the husband's area) are currently also performed by outside workers. Education and economic changes have spurred an increase in the study of detailed specialised materials and publications, which has expanded the exposure of both sexes to areas until recently under the authority of the other, such as mechanical repairs, food preparation, and business dealings.

Everyone wishes to form a materially integrated family unit after marriage, but individuals in the modern age are more free to marry someone without much regard as to whether that person will offer supplements to the household. The individual assumes that the new household will be 'complete', in that all domestic functions will be adequate; food, clothing, cleaning and so on are already up to par, because outside workers provide the services. The only exception to this rule, the only supplement that is desired, is the *extra income which the spouse can contribute*, which can be used to obtain the necessary goods and services.

Finally, the youth culture is a separate force that encompasses, in effect, the first two independent variables, and contributes to the increase in similarity. Although selfishness is often associated with youth, dependence on others, although expected, is not in keeping with the modern aspiration for autonomy. This desire for autonomy was discussed in Sporer (2010B), and that study showed that, because of the complex effects of household structure, culture, and economic factors, many people living in modern industrialised societies might believe that it is impossible to have 'freedom' and be married at the same time. Consequently, there is a potential inability to both give love and receive love at the same time. Young people are emblematic of the free, unconstrained spirit, and 'complete' autonomy for adults involves having the same casual cross-sex relations as adolescents.

Many aspects of the preoccupation with staying young have gained a certain seductiveness in America, and possibly partly due to this, a desire for equality between the sexes has arisen.[21] There is, in this case, little need for differentiation between the sexes, i.e. they generally have the same responsibilities and rights, and if the 'eternal youth' paradigm is to flourish, there must be little to differentiate the sexes even in adulthood. To assign different complex roles to each sex would be to destroy the illusion of 'staying young' mentally and physically. However, these ideas are not limited to America, but have become accepted elsewhere. By virtue of cultural diffusion, other nations, neither as industrially advanced nor as modernist, have obtained and even amplified the concepts described above.

Unfortunately, arrangements can be hindered by the independence ethos, where people often believe that they can handle a challenge in their own way, without assistance, direction or education. Independence creates a storehouse of experiences upon which one can build competence and social rank, but it is not 'sociable' in the sense that a companion or spouse is prevented from gaining a whole view of one's personality. Instead of calling for this curtain, this veil, to be removed, so that openness and cooperation might be possible, society has moved to keep it in place whilst putting increasing emphasis on making similarity the cornerstone of the 'happy' marriage. Such an interference in free decision-making makes courtship difficult and marriage potentially volatile.

Thus, we see that preserving harmony within the male-female relationship, in particular of the marital type, has become increasingly difficult, due to an abandonment of traditional European concepts, and an acceptance of modern self-centred ideas related to a desire for 'independence'. Let us now examine further the methods that modern society has implemented as purported solutions to the problem of unsatisfying marriages.

Chapter 5

Modern Simplifications

*S*ociety has, over time, secured many advancements in comfort, health, and convenience. Yet, it has accomplished far less in bringing the issues of selfishness and dependence into the forum of public discourse. In spite of the average person's clear knowledge of the issues, society has chosen not to encourage discussions of the matter; public forums have therefore remained silent. Over an extended period of time—from great-grandparent, to grandparent, to parent, to the present—anxieties have steadily grown about the ability to perform complex roles in home life. Perhaps the operative word in this case should be 'willingness', and not 'ability', because it is not that people lack the mental and physical resources, but rather that they are not prepared to make the sacrifices in fully assuming their responsibilities. This anxiety, or rather this guilt, has been lessened, if not expiated, because of explanations offered by one branch of the same Revolution that initially gave rise to this guilt. 'Science' maintained that the traditional solution for every marital problem, which was to put aside selfish attitudes and *work hard for respect* within the context of household life, was an untenable idea in the face of the enlightened conclusion that human beings were destined to act and think only within the *narrow* guidelines set down by Nature. In the modern age, many think that the completely happy married couple, of course, were in reality a coincidence, an accident, and never the result of diligent dedication. It is no coincidence, however, that the rise of the modernist independent lifestyle was accompanied by the florescence of institutional science, from which people could easily procure this deterministic explanation of human relations as a way of excusing their own tardiness in changing for the better. As evidence mounted that genetics played a role in animal behaviour, many were tempted to see the same role in human actions. These observations were built on age-old beliefs, many correct, that inheritance in humans had a strong influence on certain basic elements of behaviour, such as shyness. However, these ideas were taken one step further, in that the 'influences' became 'causes'; it was thought that people were hidebound in acting out the programme that nature had assigned to them, a sensational but ultimately counterfeit and tragic idea. Indeed, scientists became convinced that ideal marriages were no longer made in heaven, but in the genetic code.

Public discussions about the 'natural' impulses of human beings could not be contained to only one area. The same need for 'separation' between different social and ethnic groups that spawned the Eugenics movement and the racialism of the 20th century, also lies behind the ethos that 'incompatible' marriages must be ended.[22] It was thought that if at all possible, such unions should never be established in the first place. Thus, like and like must be brought together because it is the way of Nature, an argument not easily refuted. The same thinking is responsible for the great social interest in matching attributes, such as background, education, and age.

It is in the last attribute, because of its fundamental nature, that we can see at work a critical part of the modern marital strategy that we have yet to discuss in detail, that of *simplification*. In the struggle to find similarity in a potential spouse, people have attempted to simplify the process by routinely matching overt traits such as age, whilst neglecting a deeper examination of temperament and personality. These ideas are grounded on the belief in distinct phases of life bringing different attitudes, challenges, behaviours and responsibilities. It would therefore make sense that a person from an 'early' phase of life should not marry someone from the 'late' phase.

Obtaining someone's age is probably the attribute most easily obtained; it requires only a simple question or observation. And by the same token, when this attribute is matched between husband and wife, it is the most easily determined of any homology. We can see that reducing a persona's complexity to a simple marker, such as age, although highly attractive, threatens the courtship and marriage processes.

Universal classifications of marriage age are used by all societies to assist people in demarcating the different attitude areas that underlie marriage. In the Western world, about one in four of any population can marry 'late', that is, well past the average age; about one in four in any population can marry early, with women being more likely to do so. Many believe the terms 'early' and 'late' signify deviations from the *customary norm,* and not mere departures from an actual mathematical average or typical age. From this outlook, we can say that in most Western nations, marrying under the age of 20 is definitely 'early', and marrying over the age of 35 is definitely 'late'. Late marriage, as a traditional concept, can be defined as a first marriage where husbands are over age 26 and wives are over age 23.[23] Although this applies to the period from the 16th to the 19th centuries, it might not really hold for earlier periods, such as the Middle Ages, or later periods, such as the 20th century.

Hence, 'traditional' is a term which is derived from the early modern period, and practises should not be construed as going back to time immemorial. Furthermore, this definition becomes relativistic when it is grounded on actual averages, not expectations. A nation with an average age of 19 could see 'late' marriage as 23, or if the average were 25, then 'late' marriage could be considered 30. In more recent times, with the average age for men and women around 25, early marriage can occur before age 22, late marriage can realistically be characterised as occurring after age 30. Such opinions are always to a certain extent impressionistic, relating more to concepts of propriety rather than strict mathematical principles.

Historically, age was only a *starting* point in the marriage evaluation process, not as an absolutely reliable indicator of traits, although a different attitude finds resounding endorsement today. If age of marriage does have a major effect on marital stability, then what is 'early' or 'late' has much to do with social forces that help or hinder the success of such unions. However, we notice that although matching of age is highly attractive to many people, there are still factors that override it. The proportion of marriages in North America with a large discrepancy in age between husband and wife has declined, and the proportion with nearly the same age has increased. However, the proportion of marriages where the wife is older than the husband has not changed much.[24] This demand for homology in ages applies to first marriages, and is somewhat less strong in subsequent marriages,[25] with the trend not being the same across all age groups. Marriages were increasingly homologous in age from 1921 until 1971, but thereafter less so. From the 1920s until the 1960s, younger men tended to select brides from their own age groups, whereas from the 1940s to the 1970s, older men had marriages that were increasingly dissimilar. Although the pattern for women is not clear, women under the age of 20 tend to select older grooms.[26] These patterns follow long trends, making it unlikely that economic forces were solely responsible.

It is clear that over the course of generations, people have become more accepting of the belief, rightly or wrongly, that age is a significant determinant in personality development. We should emphasise that a married couple of disparate ages might still be quite similar to one another in personality and attitudes; the homophily between partners of the same age might be great, but compensating factors could intervene so that a great similitude between an older husband and young wife, for example, might also be enjoyed. Nonetheless, people now invest fewer resources in finding a suitable mate, putting their faith in only a hazy evaluation of attributes, a 'thumbnail sketch' of a real person.

Yet, what is not obvious is why there should be an increasing tendency in the modern age for *older* men to marry women not only from their own age group, but from other age groups as well. The general traits older women possess appeals to many older men, but other older men find that younger women offer more appealing characteristics. We can understand why young men select women close to their own age: General similarity in attributes and the availability of large pools of single females. The older man's apparent violation of the homology principle might reveal to us more about the underlying processes at work in the new marital strategy.

In the past, one reason why large age disparities among married couples were unremarkable might have had to do with accessibility in age groups. If eligible people are not present in one's age group (one's birth cohort plus or minus five years) then one would move outside of it. If marriage within a particular age group is essential, a large surplus of females always carries the certainty that many of them, although willing, cannot marry. If such marriage is *not* essential, then people who are 'shut out' of their own age group, either because of number differences or attitudes, will, if they are able, move outside of their age group, and marry people significantly older or younger than themselves.

What happens when similarity in attributes remains a dominant factor, but men can marry freely either in their own age group or outside of it? It is reasonable to assume that if older men and younger men can both relate to younger females, it is the women who then change more over time compared to men. Obviously, these older men find something more appealing about younger women and/or less appealing about women in their own age group. If it is true that people, in general, desire greater similarity from a spouse, then it would appear that *single men change less than single women as they age, thus older single men would be closer in attributes to younger single women than older single women.* What do older men and younger men have in common with younger women? To put it another way, what is the main divergence between younger and older women? Based on our previous discussions, we can divide the pertinent areas of interest into work, dependence, maturity and general personality.

Young women and young men (18 to 25 years of age) are less likely to have a full-time job than older men and women (35 to 50 years of age); however, there is little to suggest that young women are less likely to work than young men. In the second area, that of dependence, younger people are clearly more likely to be dependent than older people, but young women are only somewhat more likely to be dependent on parents and others than young men. Older single men and women are both likely to be self-reliant.

In the case of maturity, younger people undeniably have less capability in handling matters than older people, with not much difference between the sexes. For younger women, choosing an older male has traditionally meant more stability, a more mature partner that would balance out the woman's lack of knowledge, naivete and emotionality. On the other hand, many older men still favour older women due to their maturity and ability to function as full partners in the marriage. Indeed, many younger men desired older women for the same reasons. However, whereas older women and older men are similar in experiences and maturity, we find that younger females and older males are fairly similar in personality and perceptions.[27] Let us now see why this would be.

We note that in the area of personality (habits and interests) there is a considerable contrast between women of different ages. Young women are much more likely to engage in activities that are typically *male*, such as in the areas of clothing, sports, language, and entertainment, with the result that young men and young women enjoy the greatest intersection of interests of any combination of age groups. The easy acceptance of girls crossing over to engage in 'tomboy' activities stands in great contrast to the prohibitions boys encounter in trying to do 'girlish' things. In fact, whilst most women have engaged in activities that are typically male, the few boys who do engage in typically female activities are seen as having 'behavioural problems'. Although boys become somewhat less masculine with age, *girls show a greater increase in feminine habits, so that the gap between the two sexes increases with age.*[28] Even women who are in their late teens and early 20s probably betray more willingness to engage in male activities than older women. There are many advantages to knowing both sex roles from the inside, so to speak, as one is then less likely to feel uncomfortable or confused in a situation where the opposite sex predominates. It would appear women use the generous free time of youth to discover the world of male activities, even when occasionally thwarted by domineering boys who see this as an incursion into their domain. As adults, women must decisively take on clear feminine characteristics, which conversely means abandoning certain masculine ones. We can conclude that *younger women and men, of any age, are therefore relatively close to each other in regards to social activity and role responsibilities.*

Similarity in personality, in general, usually demands little change from a spouse, but it does not guarantee a smooth transition into other areas of life after marriage, if the *roles* of husband and wife are significantly different. Thus, although we do not minimise the significance of similarity in attributes in choosing a mate, partners of different ages, despite noticeable divergence in personality, might have to *undergo less of a change* in certain ways than similarly aged partners. Men often experience less of a change between single life and married life, as they still have the roughly the same attitudes and behaviour in both lifestyles. Women usually undergo a greater change; to give one example, they usually give up their jobs in order to raise children. As a result, a younger woman, who has still not grown into the habit of being a member of the labour force, will find the transition easier than for older women. For this reason, many older men in the latter half of the 20th century have found it necessary to override the advantages of marrying an older woman by marrying a younger one. If people prefer *minimal shifting* of responsibilities between the single life and married life, then dissimilarity is as important as similarity.

We can see that when fluency and ease of social relations are important, *men and women will seek others of the same age.* But when a strong, masculine response to external challenges is critical, then the older woman, despite her maturity, does not inspire the passions of an older (or younger) man. A more masculine type wife, perhaps a 'tomboy', is desired when social pressures escalate. For this reason, the two persons will likely come from different age groups. Still, *homology* between the man and woman is stressed: Similarity in general attributes in the age-matching scenario, but similarity in more specific attributes in the age-diverse scenario. It is apparent that one dynamic can actually explain two opposite tendencies. The strong desire for similarity, and thus for simplicity, explains why some people prefer to marry people in their same age group; on the other hand, the desire for reinforcement and balance leads others to prefer marrying members of different age groups.

In the present social circumstances, the focus is now on *having a wife who is more masculine*, and consequently less feminine, and who requires less assistance in the transition from single to married life. Extensive changes in the set of characteristics that the average older man finds desirable forced a shift in focus; *now the younger, stronger, assertive, effervescent, girl–woman becomes the preferred wife*, eclipsing the advantages the older woman has to offer. This kind of woman, who has become a prototypical wife in many societies, is the product of the modern *simplification dynamic* of male-female relationships. As long as husband and wife have the same general interests, and as long as certain fundamental personality traits are the same (such as strength and eagerness), whatever major differences exist in disposition, might be tolerable as long as each has the opportunity to adequately express their distinctive qualities without attempts at suppression or criticism.

As we stated earlier in the chapter, although age is an easily determined 'natural' factor that is commonly used for predicting a wide array of traits, it is by no means all-encompassing; the factors related to age are important, but there are others that must also be taken into account. Hence, this change in marriage pattern results not from the appearance of a new basic paradigm, but from a broadening of long-standing ideas that in the past were widely held, albeit not often put into practise. What some men once only fancied or dreamt about, they now demand.

From the general perspective, we can observe that the differences in traits or behaviour between people have become more irksome. Even where certain people seek out differences in a spouse for practical purposes of compensation, there is the probability that, in the emotional domain, the divergence in personalities might create a sense of incompleteness to the relationship. The tolerance, indeed the necessity, of differences between spouses has become undone by the individual aversion to making a major sacrifice in personality.

It is, at first glance, not apparent whether there are now more differences, or a greater latitude of differences, than in the past, although this would be unimportant if the *level* of tolerable difference remained the same. Within this desire for similarity, is an all-important move *away from complementarity*, with a loss of profundity and depth in a relationship, and thus less fulfilment.

Even in the span of a generation, the way people think about marriage has changed substantially. A study of matrimonial advertisements, wherein people described what they wanted in a suitable spouse. Over a 35-year period, the differences between what men deemed desirable in women, and what women deemed desirable in men, *diminished* considerably. Married life slowly became a 'place' where the couple hope there will be mutual emotional satisfaction, and not so much a genuine partnership where *complementarity* of interests was of major concern.[29] What 'satisfaction' means is unclear when constructive heterology is removed from the concept of the successful companionate relationship.

Chapter 6

The Narrowing of
Married Life

*B*ased on the strength of the evidence we have considered up to this point, we may conclude that modern couples want to both reduce the *number* of differences between partners, and to reduce the *depth* or *extent* of each difference. Moreover, we have seen that people have difficulty confronting their inability to see the advantages of positive complementarity, and their use of differences, such as in age, in fundamentally selfish ways. It is clear that the dynamics of marriage and family life in the modern age have become greatly *narrowed* or constricted, preventing the constructive, richer, more profound aspects of human existence to enter into the daily activities of ordinary people.

The great institution that, for centuries, has been a magnificent jewel in our Western culture treasury, is now reduced to a greatly simplified 'product' that is shallow, cold, sterile, and unappealing. Because of economic competition, geographic dislocation, negation of traditions, and confusion over moral values, people now utilise short-term strategies, and fluctuate between inflexible egotism on the one hand, and immature dependence on the other, relinquishing opportunities for constructive mutual enhancement. Such distancing behaviours unquestionably make intimacy 'cheaper' in terms of emotional cost, but by weakening and degrading individuality, the relationship has far less of an ability to deliver special rewards.

Thus, the idea of marriage as being unlike any other relationship has given way to the idea of an affiliation as only moderately differentiated from others, and increasingly similar, in its various parameters, to ordinary leisure and business friendships. In the wake of the millions rushing to use the 'exit door' of divorce, marriage has become much like any other group, where the *uniqueness*, and hence the distinct attractiveness, of the relationship has vanished. This is not to say married life is the same as unmarried life, for the two will always remain distinct entities requiring different roles and obligations. But where before marriage was indissoluble, now it is 'partible' like any business relationship. Where intimate ideas were once passed only between husband and wife, now even co-workers tell each other extremely personal information. These changes have inspired an increased insistence on ideological solidarity, particularly when couples feel compelled (from media influences or otherwise) to detail activity from a much broader spectrum. The special maturity and considerations that the marital union used to demand have fallen by the wayside, and now the couple accept the same pitfalls and weaknesses as found in any other 'dyad'.

However, the preeminent capacity of married life to turn dissimilarity from a deficit into a strength has not been lost. Some of our ancestors, no doubt, might have had little in common in terms of temperament and interests, but they had a satisfying life because each partner conscientiously contributed his or her own unique resources to a secure, well-run household, where there were emotional assets, financial resources, good child-care, and communal stability. Today, complementarity, at least without overriding homophily, is ignored if not rejected.

In such an environment, men and women will often not see the realities of a relationship, and self-deception is common. Couples stress concord in various areas, such as politics, spending habits, religion, leisure, children, and careers because they are dependent on solidarity in order to survive. They might accept that certain superficial factors match, but refuse to see that deeper and more pervasive factors do not. Research shows that young couples put great emphasis on consensus and agreement, but agreement in real life is often much *lower* than thought.[30]

This deception clearly presents problems. Notwithstanding the many advantages to homology, to press for it socially is in many cases undesirable. The idea of similarity in attitudes, when too forcefully implemented, creates *fewer options* in people's lives, which in turn creates frustration, psychological impairment, and instability. The evidence shows that, whilst similarity within marriage is, in general, a good thing, it should not be imposed but be allowed to arise in a natural manner, with people freely coming together because of congruence of temperament, education, interests, and occupation. Without this organic development, the marriage, no matter how opulent the ceremony or how widely disseminated the announcement, is totally *inauthentic*.

Certain psychological factors have a primary role in fulfilling or denying conceptual models of the family household. There is nothing in any one of these factors that, in and of itself, actually is a physical obstacle to matrimony and forming a family. The modern world presents enough economic opportunities for forming even the most basic household, far more than in the past, where men and women in many, though by no means all, cases had to depend on inheritance for marriage. Thus, the situations and developments discussed here are perhaps not surprising, as the situation in which married people find themselves arises out of a matrix that nourishes sometimes very different cultures and backgrounds, all made largely possible by migration and economic development. In the era of individual freedom and materialism, which has in many ways catalysed geographic movement, families have taken to disassembling social traditions as they see fit. There cannot be a reversal of this depreciation of marriage, except when people come to live in *culturally homogeneous regions*, or when people pay more attention to the characteristics of the person they intend to marry. The latter approach at the present time seems more feasible, although not necessarily likely to happen.

In the modern age, so many people hold to the concept that one finds 'fulfilment' only through a 'compatible' marriage, within which the expected attitudes are a low willingness to change, and an intolerance of diversity. We must ask: How has Western culture allowed the emergence of a viewpoint that is so narrow—indeed, one could say, parsimonious and barely sufficient?

Adding to our prior discussions on the industrial economy, we shall presently examine in detail how numerous external demands on one's affiliation and attention, as a function of business and commerce, have impacted the ability of the family to bring love and gratification into the lives of its members. Although both males and females have changed their attitudes and behaviours, causing a reduction in *connubium's* ability to fulfill, the story of the loss of affection is really one that centres on *changes in the concept of home life*, although not necessarily in the marriage *ideal*. The activity and structure of the family were forced to undergo several revisions, and the role most affected by this would be the one which deals with most of the details of household, namely that of the wife.

After we review historical developments, it will become apparent why so many consider marriage an 'institution under threat': It is because the institution has been *reconstructed*, with positive womanhood removed, and all of the ignoble elements of the masculine sex worked into the structure, weakening it to the point where it verges on collapse. Accordingly, womanhood, or the *feminine,* would be the subject of transformation, with the masculine undergoing less change.[31] We already alluded earlier to an aspect of this dynamic, by demonstrating that older men find it important to marry younger women who are 'tough' and 'strong', characteristics not in keeping with the feminine (see page 55).

Let us start by saying, that it is difficult to know how people define roles, no more than in the past, when even the concept of 'role' was entirely connected to occupation and status. For example, there could be no mother or father role without authority being inherent in these positions. Although the nobility expected equality in the level of authority between husband and wife, such equality was lacking in the social schema; the noble family itself was considered superior to that of lower echelon families. This differentiation was accepted by all orders of society, because along with the superior status of the nobility came extraordinary responsibilities. Hence, as a group, the highest authority rested with the nobility, who also therefore saw themselves embodying the *apotheosis* of a role, be it as mothers, fathers, children, siblings, uncles, aunts, men or women. Moreover, as the nobility had the time, the education, and a definite necessity for defining their various roles, we could look to them for legitimate insight as to how Western man in general perceives the masculine and feminine. Most importantly, since they had the opportunity to live life, pretty much any way they wanted, freed from toiling and manual labour, freed from most material constraints except attending to official protocols, the nobility could conceive of the ideal without prejudice, as a product of the refined intellect. In short, the life of the nobleman was to be the standard by which everyone should live. Naturally, this type of life was a prototype that not everyone could achieve, no matter how wealthy.

Nonetheless, ideals about family life were procured by the middle and lower classes from elite purveyors, although how much of an influence on behaviour they had is something that has to be determined. The ruling class apparently had genuine insight into these ideals, and did not merely propagate an arbitrary standard meant to preserve their power. They did peer deep into themselves and their culture to see the true nature of the masculine and feminine, of family life, the home, the ultimate 'centre of power'.

What the nobility found in their enquiries was that being a member of the elite meant not only being superior materially, but also *morally and ethically*. Women, in particular, were expected to perpetuate all the best traits of humanity. Consequently, this meant that women should possess a wide variety of attributes, talents, viewpoints, and perspectives. In this way, they could exhibit compassion, discipline, intelligence, and honesty; they had to show great foresight, discussing openly these matters, and diligently pursuing the ideal. We can see that in the traditional period the wise man would seek a wife who had *great diversity* of traits. Most women emphasised virtue, and pursued a course that was meant to promote warmth and affection. Regnant in the domestic but not public sphere, subordinated to men in many ways, these women nonetheless held interrelated strands of psychological and spiritual power, all inextricably tied to being a member of the nobility.[32]

However, it is most important to understand that this complex expression of the virtues was not tied to being married, having children, or any other specific social arrangement. The women of the past were very conscious of the role that they played, more so than men and other classes in society, and so were instrumental in promoting the ideals embodied within that role. The goal of this pattern of behaviour was to *safeguard affection* between men and women, an ideal that was often mentioned but not very often met. In many ways, the ideal noblewoman was not very different from the model of the Christian saint, except that the former had certain temporal powers and responsibilities that the latter often did not. Perhaps it is somewhat contradictory to expect noblewomen to produce and raise heirs to keep the family name, and at the same time to promote chastity. In the same way, it is difficult to epitomise modesty and humility when being attended by courtiers and servants, whilst wearing splendid, perhaps opulent, garments. Nonetheless, obeying male social precepts, tightly controlling household affairs, setting the standard for morality, submission to worthy endeavours, were connected to the ideal concept of the 'feminine'.

We cannot easily separate these factors, and few women, no matter how latitudinarian, have tried; that is, until the 20th century. Although being called on to produce children, women in general were ideally thought to be removed from the world, taking care of the household, a place of the 'now', without past or future, a place of security and care. Social and natural circumstances would come and go, but noblewomen continued to be the protectors of the important things in life, of the things that have longevity and solidity. It did not really matter whether a woman was married or had children in order to live this ideal. The key responsibility that the ideal woman had was to skilfully arrange and organise the items and forces that were present in the household, to bring to completion the mission that God had assigned to her, after giving consideration to the needs and limitations of her personality. Where men were concerned with the transitory nature of business and politics, women cared for the things of the home, which indeed have remained unchanged far longer than anything in the 'male' world outside.

Whatever the success or urgency in implementing these ideas, the Industrial Revolution did not allow these highly important psychological and spiritual mechanisms to continue. The public at that time were called upon to make sacrifices, not for God or home, but for industry, unions, and military. Many entities now demanded time and money; sometimes a person had to surrender his own life in the service of a 'cause'. Perhaps not surprisingly, along with this excessive exertion, there was an increase in deviant behaviours, including alcoholism, illegitimacy, drug use, prostitution, membership in secret societies and occult groups, pornography, violence, riots, theft, murder, rape, and fraud.

Turmoil in society grew within the context of rapidly growing cities, factories and encroaching government authority, but in spite of the power of these burgeoning entities, no one was unable to stop the disruption. The concept of autonomy, so crucial for growing commerce, had degenerated into widespread lawlessness.

The literature of the period reveals this struggle by presenting many combinations of individuals in relationships where affection, gratification, child-rearing, and marriage became separate mental and emotional areas. Men had affairs with married women, women had children out of wedlock, women loved men, but men did not love them in return. By discussing the attractions and disadvantages of each of these configurations, it was hoped a greater understanding would emerge, and people would then be more in control of their destinies.

To keep marriage as a functioning institution, and to maintain the power that came from traditional social roles, many thought that the family structure had to change. *People understood that the last line of defence was the family,* and measures were taken by fearful individuals to counteract the threats from the outside. Anxiety over the etiolation of the ideal of marriage, as was exposed by aristocratic and noble ladies, made men and women stoically depend on *formalism* to guarantee its longevity, even if in their hearts they did not believe it would work. And the inspiration for this formalism was drawn from the environment in which they lived. The period between the early 1800s and the 1840s was a time when the public were directing their attention to the impact of technology and machinery on society, due to the demand for increased economic efficiency. Although many communities opposed mechanisation, it succeeded in pervading all aspects of life, and protests against mechanisation were met by stern governmental countermeasures. *This new society of the machine, of conflicting demands, migration, dislocation, confusion and violence, prompted a call by individuals and groups to bring strict order to the primary social unit, the household.*[33] Just as the labour unions forced workers to join their 'brothers' in a movement against exploitation, so too did the family 'union' wage a struggle against its own adversaries, whether they be ill-bred suitors, thieving servants, licentious neighbours or conniving relatives.

Thus, we can see in the mechanical workplace and the 'mechanical' family, reactions that appear companionate and virtuous, but that do not fulfill emotional needs, and that also clash with that sense of independence that comes from playing a respected role in society. Although regimentation was effective in counteracting the dangers of recklessness, it left little time for the family and little spontaneous affection between family members. The model of strict adherence to the virtues was palliated by what people saw as the realities of the day; being 'soft' was quickly becoming a vice and not an asset. Respect and honour automatically paid to virtue were dwindling, and women began to fear a loss of social position; indeed they felt that they were becoming only another 'ethnic' group clamouring for rights.[34] In this scenario, not only was emotional security being forfeited, but also independence; two highly important aspects of life were losing their vitality in spite of the onslaught of impassioned speeches and vigorous social action.

Although the emphasis on family life was welcome, the maternal domestic role was becoming the only viable one for women. Virtue and social separateness, although important, were being overwhelmed by the demands of achieving and maintaining a high standard of living and the careful upbringing of children.

It was becoming increasingly difficult, in a materialistic competitive society, to marry a person close to the ideal, someone kind, disciplined, truthful, and loyal. The changes to marriage that had taken place by the 19th century were so great as to frighten many people away from pursuing relationships outside the circle of their relatives. Homology thus became an instrument for social stability. Ideally, men and women could meet one another under the assumption that many of their ideas about marriage and family were already comparable. They could then deal more easily and thoroughly with the other problems, including employment, career, and standard of living preferences and other critical areas undergoing significant changes. This is an instance where attitudes are not entirely determined through independent reasoning, but are strongly influenced from the outside.

Serious distrust must have been quite palpable in English and other European societies during the early part of the Industrial Revolution. Communities accommodated to a certain extent this xenophobia (or was it really an unrealistic fear?). For children living in the households of the middle and upper class 'Victorian' period, everyday life was often closed to outside contact, except to relatives and close friends of the family. Often these friends themselves were related to each other. The few individuals eligible for friendship that a person might have met in adolescence would have been siblings and cousins. Since siblings were sexually *ultra vires*, but cousins were not, marriage between cousins fulfilled both the need for social duty and the personal need for emotional security. In the restricted climate of many families, one's marriage to a cousin provided a satisfying solution to the dilemma of how to live an socially acceptable life, and still avoid the awkward difficulties of discovering a suitable, respectable mate. The prevalence of marriages between cousins is not known with certainty, but in the wealthier classes it was relatively high, was possibly well above one in twenty.[35] The prevalence of such marriages tends to substantiate the concept that people married their cousins because few people apart from relatives were available, and this dearth of marriage partners existed because families restricted their social circle due to a grave suspicion of the motivations of 'outsiders'.

Marriage within the family, namely with cousins, was one convenient way for men and women to progress along the life course without undue investment or risk in the search for partners. This was especially true of busy professional men who did not wish to take time away from their business for such romantic and basically impractical enterprises. The conveyance of family wealth into dependable hands might have been another important reason for marriage between relatives. However, the main motivation for cousin marriage was grounded in a love for the familiar and safe, as a cousin would often resemble, both physically and temperamentally, a beloved parent or sibling. Falling in love with 'outsiders' was becoming too precarious, and a cousin had an easily verifiable history and background.

There was the unmistakable impression that stability and predictability in human relations were ebbing. One of the most significant books of the Victorian period, Charlotte Brontë's *Jane Eyre*, put forward a strange plot development that apparently, for the readers of the 19th century, did not strain the credibility of the work: The heroine's prospective husband turns out not only to be already married, but his wife is a disturbed, tragic figure living in the attic of his mansion. Evidently, this motif, and it was repeated in various forms in other works, resounded with people who had become highly alarmed at the shocking things that they themselves had uncovered within their own surroundings.

The practise of marriage between cousins became so prevalent that it was a matter of public debate by the mid-19th century. There were critics and as well as advocates of close relation marriage, who discussed the effects on society that this type of union would have. Both sides echoed the genetic concepts of the Eugenics movement, whose members encouraged inbreeding of superior traits, and discouraged inbreeding of inferior traits. However, this did not take into account the psychological motives of these relationships.

As love was viewed as an 'irrational' aspect to life since it did not have a practical and visible end result, the great Rationalists of the late 19th century, men who themselves were often separated from their emotions, had little choice but to invoke a 'rational' explanation for why so many people had a fervent attraction to family members, even if they could not marry them. According to the science of the time, real 'affection' did not exist. It was thought that deeply emotionally satisfying feelings about someone else, instigated only by the sharing of ideas, was a myth, and the basic goal of any intimate relationship was to satisfy sexual urges. Thus, it was only 'rational' that men would want to associate with whatever women were available, as a way of satisfying their instinctual desire.

However, this 'rational' explanation failed to address those situations where men engaged in illicit affairs, presumably to satisfy their sexual desires, but in the process transgressing society's laws. This clearly 'irrational' behaviour required other explanations. Despite the evidence from history, some psychologists invoked the theory that cousin unions were not the result of logical reactions to a changing environment, but a so-called displacement of incestuous feelings, sexual desire being shifted from a close relative to another socially acceptable relative. There is little reason to suspect that this is the case; it is far from certain that the prime reason for these marriages was a *sexual* desire for close relatives. Rather, it seems that they desired a quite understandable close but *non-sexual* relationship with family members, and that they wished, if possible, to continue it in some form into adulthood. The love of a father might prompt a young girl to marry her cousin not because she wishes another father per se, but because she wishes to maintain the same type of constructive relationship with her husband that she had had with her father in childhood and adolescence. This is especially true if the father died young or was away from the household most of the time. Sporer (2010B) investigated this phenomenon of how the loss of affection and guidance in the home of childhood can lead to an increase in marriage tendency in adulthood. Hence, close attachment to relatives was more a function of the desire for emotional security and continuity, rather than secret forbidden sexual obsessions.

The issue of closeness between members of a family, not surprisingly, entered into the discussions between doctors and patients, giving shape to the burgeoning sexualisation theories of human nature, the most well-known of which was Freud's Oedipal complex. Whatever problems arose in life could be traced back to the way in which people dealt with or did not deal with this underlying sexual longing.

We can see in these developments the beginning of the substitution of sex for affection in relationships. Close affiliation between relatives was thought by many scientists to be nothing more than a rather vain attempt to live out a fantasy incestuous affair with someone that resembled a parent in physical appearance and/or in personality. Nonetheless, it is far more in keeping with the evidence to say that people cultivated deep friendships with close relations exactly as a way to *negate* or defuse the issue of sexuality.

In time, all male-female affection became linked in some way with the 'basic' instinctual urge of sexual attraction. Sexuality was seen as the unalterable basis for almost all kinds of intimate human interactions, and it was thought that this 'beast' was especially difficult to tame when people of the opposite sex, of similar age and background, were together unchaperoned.

By late 19th century, scientists were of the opinion that the 'healthy' male, as an expression of natural instinctual forces, sought out sexual intimacy on a regular basis. However, this 'healthy' desire brought unwelcome situations to society, since it meant that men would be seeking sex from unmarried women and prostitutes in order to satisfy their desires, with result of numerous out-of-wedlock pregnancies, abortions, and cases of venereal disease. Only within the marital relationship could the negative social consequences of sexual desire be avoided. Yet, even within marriage, many thought that sexuality, precisely because of its 'instinctual basis', might threaten the emotional relationship between husband and wife. Since experts identified certain intimate male-female relationships, such as between cousins or siblings, as being based not on love and affection but on male sexual desires, then by extension the marital relationship itself could very well be nothing more than an outlet for the husband's sexual urges.

Alternatively, since sexual intimacy between relatives such as brother and sister was socially unacceptable, a loving, respectful, affectionate, and mutually supporting tie between siblings became ever more essential. It *freed* the individual from having to worry about how to proceed in his emotional life; marriage, sex, childbirth, establishing family, were all removed from the equation. The spectre of the 'carnal' was safely contained within the marriage of ordinary life, and the various unconventional liaisons of literature.

What none of the supposed experts and authorities could see was that the sudden importance of these intensely intimate relationships between family members were not caused by instinctual urges, but rather were caused by a changing environment that made people search for *effective solutions* to a difficult new world. Thus, the search for homology in companionate relationship led in a twisting path to a place where a number of social and scientific programmes branched off to assault traditional wisdom.

We should stress, that the narrowing of the social circle and the turn to family members for friends and spouses, in an attempt to bring security to one's life, were in no way irrational or pathological. Indeed, these were logical reactions to a complex situation that confronted ordinary people not only with challenges that were unforseen, but that were not soluble using inherited concepts. It is perhaps not so much the case that these relationships became more numerous, but rather, that the other types of relationships, of men and women meeting and marrying non-family members, became more rare.

Chapter 7

The Change in the Ideal

Critical social struggles are often waged against a background of major transformation of personal life, and this principle was certainly active in the Western world of the late 19th century, where societies endeavoured to create a structure that could both tolerate traditional standards, and at the same time, support the growth of the industrial economy. Indubitably, the demand for similarity and simplicity in marital relationships created changes in the relationship between men and women. The damage that has occurred to the psyche is in the critical 'interface' between individual and society, arising out of an imbalance between individual need and social need. When such damage is done, both love and independence as major goals in life become unreachable. Further, marriage was negatively affected by downgrading of the complexities of love to simplified biological and physical factors. As the 20th century approached, many people were becoming increasingly uncomfortable with the prospect of marriage and family. The methods used to remove the uncertainty about people, as discussed in the previous chapter, were not enough is assuaging people's fears. Thus, more drastic changes in psychology began to occur, which affected the ideal of marriage itself. These changes impacted women more than men, because order and control over the resources of private life, which gave women the power to choose cooperative and considerate marriage partners, were dwindling.

What is this mental change in the period we are discussing? We note that in recent times personal antipathy is the likely cause of a delay in marriage, whereas previous generations often did not marry due to an external economic agency. However, firm, logical statements about what women found wrong with men, marriage, family, and children have been uncommon, and instead we see the increasing use of psychological devices that allow indirect avoidance of responsibility. Hence, there is evidence that this antipathy towards marriage was based on a reaction to an *unarticulated and undifferentiated fear of something in the social environment*. We need to precisely state the feelings and thoughts that were concealed during this important period in Western history.

It is, upon examination of the attitudes of ordinary people and professionals of the time, easy to see what was feared by these women. Life had become subject to more *rigid rules* than ever before, where even the duties of wife and mother merited scientific and public scrutiny. By the 1890s, child-rearing needed to be standardised as well, and not surprisingly evolved into having a 'scientific' and 'professional' appearance. The individual was increasingly losing his or her personal freedom, ironically at a time when freedom was supposed to be on the ascendency. How was love supposed to flourish and be maintained in such an environment?

Marriage was losing its appeal as a unique place where both husband and wife could both find fulfilment through mutual support and enhancement. Although this was possible with the people of the traditional period, those of the 19th century found they could not re-connect to these principles. The aversion to growing up, sex, and pregnancy were closely tied to losing the bond of intimacy, as the 'pragmatic' idea of having a marriage where sex predominated over affection was intolerable. Women reacted to this by succumbing to their first natural reaction: Reject marriage and childbirth. They wished to find happiness in purely non-sexual intimacy with family members, or if necessary, no intimacy at all. There is much to indicate that such a desire for chaste love was common, but *the pressure to conform to social dicta about marriage, children, and domestic roles was overwhelming*. Intuitively, we know that anytime large numbers of people pull away deliberately from fulfilling the ideal of companionate love, some kind of damage has occurred to the average person's psyche.

Nonetheless, many felt that the only way out of the dilemma was through radical means. Some women wanted to remove the equality with men that the modern age had pronounced, and revert to a secondary status, where the responsibilities of adulthood did not have to be met. This avoidance of adulthood cannot, of course, be achieved through legal means, as everyone who reaches the age of 18 is considered to be fully mature. However, adulthood can be forestalled if one is not fully formed in the physical domain. Hence, a woman could maintain a child-like status and render herself unsuitable as a wife by inducing secondary amenorrhoea. The only way such an effect could be reliably accomplished was by losing enough weight so as to cease menses, and so to produce a 'second childhood'. Far from being a very recent disorder, self-starvation, or anorexia nervosa as it came to be called, was first noted around the year 1800, with the first professional discussion about the subject being held in 1873. This disease appeared in France by 1892, where it was ostensibly tied to the goal of attaining a slim 'glamourous' figure, possibly a preoccupation with superficiality of appearance. Nonetheless, even early on, self-starvation was connected with a definite intention to avoid entering adulthood. Those girl with the disorder explained that, in an effort to evade the onerous responsibilities they felt were present in marriage, they wished in some way to maintain their childhood; a more fanciful way to put it was that they simply wanted to fall sleep and wake up grown old.[36] In the first two decades of the 20th century, doctors in Switzerland associated the disorder with a desire to regress mentally; by making themselves very thin, girls end not only ovulation but also their physical maturity, which in turn obviates marriage and childbirth. The inability of these girls to weigh the myriad arguments for or against marriage was symbolically rendered as psychological paralysis that was often associated with anorexia.

The implication to these psychological issues is that the natural outcome of love, which is genuine companionate marriage, could never be reached; the individual found herself in limbo. If writers are allowed to some extent to articulate the most disturbing thoughts circulating in society, then perhaps Oscar Wilde's observation on matrimony was revelatory: 'One should always be in love. That is the reason one should never marry'.[37]

In many respects, these ideas about of 'correct' behaviour multiplied, ironically with a parallel increase in contradictions in standards. A multiplicity of ideas is often beneficial, but in the 19th century it led to a confusion of standards, clashes of concepts between regions, generations, and social classes. In the late 19th century, the changes initiated by the Industrial Age created a double-stress phenomenon. On the one hand, domestic work had become less interesting and less rewarding, but on the other hand, this work demanded greater expertise and proficiency. The accomplishments of men and women in the outside world of business and science outshone and trivialised the 'quaint' role of housewife.

Naturally, at first this anxiety was not articulated but was felt, as many people saw marriage become an increasingly precarious enterprise. People were demanding that ideas and standards be similar, but at the same time, a swelling diversity of expectations and commitments greater than at any point in the history of Western civilisation offered enormous challenges.

Science was called upon to end the commotion, to provide the light that would lead the individual out of 'darkness'. The destination brought on something of a shock, however, as society began to seriously alter the family paradigm. This constitutes a 'strange history' in the education and socialisation of women.[38] Physicists, doctors, chemists, and other professionals were careful to delineate the special demands of their occupations from that of the mere 'housewife', without forgetting the key role she still had to play in maintaining a living environment for a husband and children. Due to the fact that many women went to school or worked, they could no longer learn domestic skills by apprenticeship to their mothers. Now these skills were taught in the schools, and magazines, books and other materials were published as guides for women.

Women in the modern age were put upon to be experts at being wives, experts at motherhood, and experts at teaching. And all this with hardly any training at all! Such onerous duties necessitated that the household be reduced in size. Fewer children meant more attention and resources could be given to each child, thus making education more efficient. It also meant more time was available for being with one's spouse, and also greater freedom for outside work due to less time needed for domestic tasks.

One young mother from Indiana voiced the apprehension common to many in the 1920s when she said, 'Life was simple for my mother. . . . In those days one did not realize that there was so much to be known about the care of children. I realize that I ought to be half a dozen experts, but I am afraid of making mistakes and usually do not know where to go for advice'.[39] This was at a time when the childless rate for couples was at its peak, and there was the demand on women to further education and careers. Initially, this meant using a simple model where one lived one role, but forewent marriage and the others, but it eventually became common to use a model that integrated marriage, parenthood and career.

It is in one area of married life in particular that made women lose much of their independence. During the 'maturation' phase of the modern era, the idea became firmly impressed that the actual *mission* in the life of the woman was that of *motherhood*. G. Stanley Hall wrote an influential work called *Adolescence*, published in 1904, which although it contained much erroneous information, at the very least propagated certain critical concepts that would become part of the new simplified ideal of marriage. Women, in this worldview, could never find true fulfilment without becoming wives and mothers; indeed, a woman's 'body and soul are made for maternity'. A basic, innate need to take care of children, their own or others, through birth, adoption, teaching, etc., lies at the heart of the feminine. In a society that allowed men and women to fraternise, Hall worried about women becoming too masculinised and losing sight of their 'true' nature. It should come as no surprise that he also strongly urged women not remain permanently celibate and not to marry late.[40]

In a mixture of fact and fiction, Hall said publicly what many said privately. The ideal of 'love' was made easier by entirely excising affection, which was the expression of love in its most potent form. Women did actually gain some power over their lives by indisputably emphasising a unique domain: Their reproductive role. However, emotional satisfaction, unless tied to a biological function, is not part of this lifestyle, and probably cannot even be achieved. Some of the more traditional females ironically saw this new 'role' as slipping several steps down, a degeneration from the time when women had true power. The new woman was acting more the 'rustic' than the peasants ever did, a prototype hardly advanced enough to meet the demands of the new age.

There is a major theme we have pursued in this book, that complex social developments called for a major *homogenisation* and *simplification* of standards, which would restore order and defuse some of the angst surrounding married life. Although women voiced confusion over the new 'rules', their confusion was not really so much about complexity, but rather about simple knowledge. The new way of life was indeed uncomplicated and direct, but the difficulty lay in *finding an authentic source*. There had to be a narrowing of the diverse set of household forms that existed when people had a secure traditional culture, which provided what they believed were all the answers necessary for family life.

Before the Industrial Age, people had great authority and control over the *components* of their household; unlike modern people, they carefully determined and adjusted the *major* factors in their own life situation, not just rules and manners. For example, whenever couples wished to reduce instability in home life and when they wished to have more time for themselves, they reduced the number of children born into the household.

We can see this in the well-studied early modern parish of Colyton (Devon, England), where the number of children in a completed family ranged from 0 to 10, with the period 1560-1629 showing more of a tendency to cluster around the mean of about 5, than in the period 1647-1837, when more diversity in fertility was apparent. However, this diversity pertains more for women marrying under age 30, than marrying over that age.[41] As we approach the present day, this parish, like all others in England, reduced its variance in number of births. Further, the evidence shows that before the modern age, the variability in fertility from region to region, and from household to household has been extensive.[42]

Thus, the traditional household form, and by extension its rules of operation, was by no means etched in stone, and could be quite variable and changeable. The husband and wife could express their individuality within marriage, and they could quite contentedly have had many, few, or no children without an explosion of pathology requiring psychoanalysis, drugs, or group therapy.

It might be surprising to discover, that the equivalisation of womanhood with maternity is *not* a traditional idea, but a recent one, at least amongst the middle and upper classes. It is highly significant to note that in regards to an absolutely critical aspect of life, younger married women of the past were considerably different from the ones of our day in their views on children, with the latter being far more constrained in their ideals. Older married women are similar in both earlier and modern periods in their preference of having the *least* number of children possible. Being perhaps more desirous of self-development, older women preferred having more time to themselves, and were less tolerant of disruptions brought about by numerous pregnancies and children.

Therefore, by the 1880s, there is pellucid demographic evidence of a Western *standardisation* of marriage through the *homogenisation* of ideas concerning maternity, womanhood, and family life. In line with this, three cultural fertility standards were implemented in phases. In the United States, the *first standard* entailed reducing the number of families which had *high* fertility. Very large families (of 7 or more births) became much less common in the female cohort born in the 1860s (those marrying in the 1880s). This situation allowed a relatively wide latitude of behaviour: Women married, stayed or worked at home, and had children, but avoided very large numbers.

A *second standard* was then implemented with reducing of even moderate size families, the concept was circulated that anything more than *three* children was unnecessary. The rising trend in the incidence of one and two child families began with the cohort born in the 1860 to 1880s (marrying around 1880 to 1910) and evidently this trend has not yet slackened. The proportion of such families increased from about 20% in the 1880s to 63% in 1987,[43] an incredible transformation in fertility. In this scenario, as before women married and had children, but now they deliberately limited themselves to having *small families*. Theory normally determines people's behaviour, but in this period, theory about the ideal family generally *conformed* with practise, that is, behaviour came first, then attitude or opinion. The proportion of the population who believed that having two or three children was ideal rose from 64% in 1936 to 76% in 1986. However, only about half of women past their child-bearing years were actually happy with their fertility; fully one-third said they wished they had had more children.[44] This demonstrates that people *allowed the cultural ideal to be imposed on them*, at the cost of their happiness and security. They accepted an abstract idea for the good of society, but were unhappy about its implementation in their own lives.

Respect for a traditional concept, to a certain extent, was still conspicuous when women avoided having children if they were working. This is evident in the rise in the numbers of nulliparous women parallel to the rise in the number of working married women. The proportion of women not having any children began to rise in earnest in the 1860s to 1870s birth cohort (i.e. marrying 1880 to 1900), consistent with the increasingly common phenomenon of the working married woman.[45] However, the phenomenon of married women having no children peaked in the 1920s and then abated, even though married women continued to show ever greater involvement in the workforce.

Hence, the *third and final modern standard* was implemented, which reduced the acceptable number of children to two, and in addition gave women the responsibility to work outside the home. Accordingly, women married, had only two children, and worked before and sometimes during marriage.[46] This last standard created a major change in the life of the average woman, more so than the changes engendered by the previous two cultural standards. However, the ability to work not only increased one's standard of living, but also conveniently bestowed the option of divorce. Since wives could now more easily support themselves without a husband, not least because they had fewer children to raise, they could conceivably divorce their husbands and become truly independent. The sole 'mission' of women was motherhood, yet here were the means by which she could escape such a role. It is unfortunate that the advantages that women now possessed could hardly compensate for the loss of independence they suffered in the critical life area of the family, namely, sacrificing the freedom to choose celibacy if wanted; the freedom to choose one's ideal marriage partner; and the freedom to determine family size.

Today, people admit to the relevance of the third cultural standard mentioned above by saying that lower fertility is the result of wives working and the expense of raising children.[47] Interestingly, equally important but more pro-social issues now receive hardly any attention; how to raise many children in an unstable socioeconomic environment, or how to morally educate and guide children from large families, are considered either old-fashioned or eccentric questions. The present fertility model is probably one that receives wide support across social divisions, such as ethnic group, nation, class, education, region or political party. Consequently, there must be powerful fundamental reasons in support of it which makes it resilient to change. Cultural ideas about fertility are often not the result of objective examination, but social contrivances that serve the purpose of bringing a distracted society back to the critical issues in life. Having two children in marriage is the overwhelming choice of modern culture, with no differentiation between socioeconomic and demographic categories.

Thus, we see how the range of opinions about married life has been narrowed, and men and women are more likely now than in the past to court someone who has similar ideas. There is not much likelihood that men and women will find much dissimilarity between them on these fundamental issues. Whatever other divergences of attitudes exist might be reduced through the dynamics of obtaining higher education. However, as we saw in an earlier chapter, certain mechanisms found in educational system itself might work at odds with the goal of reducing diversity. We should say here that the process which discovers truth is complex and challenging. Before a deeper knowledge of society can be developed, contradictory viewpoints must be entertained before the one viewpoint that is genuinely congruent with reality can be determined. The educational system therefore encourages the putting forward of new perspectives, with the result that academics must tolerate ambiguity in the pursuit of higher understanding. However, the gaining of deeper knowledge takes time, and cannot be expected to occur within the few years that someone spends in college or university. Students are taught divergent viewpoints that usually do not resolve into a certain truth, and we can see that the modern educational system can contribute to the forming of complex adult personalities. Hence, under certain circumstances, college educated people might find it difficult to find college educated marriage partners whose views coincide with their own.

Although one might say that these changes to society were an unacceptable intrusion into very personal matters, the fact is that the standards concerning family life had to be narrowed if the industrial 'revolution' was to survive. Individuals in the modern age became unable to adjust and decide for themselves the proper family-level standards, and collective society put its 'heads together' in an attempt to determine standards for only one or two types of household. In the past, people conscientiously took the knowledge gained from family, community, and their own observations and assiduously put it into creating a personal 'culture' for their *own* version of family, adjusting this 'culture' to the size of the house-hold, whether it contained 2, 6, 10, or 17 people. These rules must have worked well, for how else can we explain the lack of percepti-ble 'family value' crises in societies with long-standing large varia-tions in household sizes and types? The modern age created a socially contrived formula to make up for a failure in individual initiative, and in this way, options became limited as did the re-wards that could be gotten from family life.

Thus, social dictates, emerging in the latter half of the 20th cen-tury and continuing to this day, are clear: Whether they like it or not, women *must* marry someone similar to themselves, marry early, and they *must* have children, but these children *cannot* num-ber more than three. Of course, one can always say, quite accu-rately, there is no formal 'law' that forces anyone to do these things, but there are informal social rules that incorporate punitive measures that are just as effective in getting compliance as those the state uses, such as the lawsuit, jail and removal of property. The ideas that society gave to women were taken because they solved immediately pressing problems, not because they brought greater contentment than older traditional ideas. Quite simply, *pragmatism is no replacement for idealism.*

From our analysis, we can reach certain conclusions. There is no doubt that principles were developed in the distant past that could help the individual balance his individual needs with social needs, within the context of family life. These principles served a highly valuable function, and can be considered part of what is known as traditional wisdom. Yet, they became untenable in a social environ-ment which put economic efficiency above all else. Over the last six or seven generations, there has been a great change in the configuration of family and married life as a result of society's unwillingness to modify economic processes in such a way so as to preserve esteemed traditional concepts. Further, European culture, which put such great emphasis on individuality and diversity of thought, could not compensate for the extraordinary demographic challenges engendered by the Industrial Revolution.

The first major social reaction to the disruptions of standards, morals, ethics and principles brought about by the Industrial Age was to *restrict the circle of people that could be considered for marriage*. Although traditionally European cultures could tolerate a wide range of ideas, these were limited by region. Those ideas which came from outside the region might possess elements whose moral qualities were unknown. The industrial age caused great movement between regions and social classes, so these situations of encountering persons of 'questionable' attitudes became common. By focussing on people within one's extended family, the frequency of such encounters was reduced, and so the likelihood of marrying a person with estimable qualities was increased.

The next major reaction was a *retreat from marriage* because of certain fears of what might happen during the course of family life: The loss of affection from a husband due to material concerns, business matters, or a mistress; the physical demands from a large number of pregnancies; the difficulties of maintaining sexual attractiveness. Even marrying someone who was well-known to the family, someone with a clear attachment to moral and ethical principles, could not guarantee happiness in marriage.

Due to these trepidations, women used various social and psychological devices to remove themselves from consideration for marriage; others wanted to delay marriage, at least until they felt mature enough to endure the problems that they feared would arise. This aversion to marriage produced great concern amongst the powerful 'caretakers' in government and academia. If such feelings widened into large patterns, society's future well-being could be threatened. Therefore, in the next social correction, the modern age began to provide a means of *establishing more control in the household*. By finding that they could *reduce fertility* in order to increase their independence by allowing time for other tasks, and to mollify their misgivings about not devoting enough time for children, women became more confident about marriage.

Interestingly, this idea of controlling fertility should have come from tradition, but it did not. As we stated earlier, couples historically had great control over their fertility, thus allowing them to bring order and uniformity over major components of their household. For some reason, this individualised authority over the number and spacing of children did not descend to the communities of the modern age.

Men and women could, in the modern age, live in a family where the option for both husband and wife to work existed, where children could be born at the time desired, and the number of children could be limited. We note that the demands incumbent upon both husband and wife were rigid, in the sense that family life no longer allowed much room for individual initiative, original thinking, or unconventional concepts. Consequently, it is clear that there had to be similarity of opinions and attitudes across a range of issues for the marriage 'situation' to work. Of course, what works in theory, 'on paper' so to speak, often does not work out in reality, if the theory is based on incorrect assumptions. Even if the plan did not work because emotional satisfaction was not achieved, then the option existed to end the marriage, and women could now even support themselves and their children, without a husband. The frequent use of this 'escape route' of divorce reveals to us that, indeed, individual estimates about the personalities of other people are often incorrect, suggesting that people are marrying not the real person, but an false image.

But what if men and women do not want to conform to the modern convention? For example, they want to marry later, marry someone of different interests, background, occupational ambitions, and education. Perhaps, they even might want to have many children. Of course, there might be social penalties, sometimes severe ones, for establishing such a relationship. The hallowed economic 'revolution' of the 19th century produced certain social standards that society today considers an integral part of that 'revolution'. Society could no more tolerate a rejection of those social standards, than it could tolerate a rejection of the Industrial Age itself. But with courage, intelligence, and diligence, two people can make such a 'non-modern' relationship work, perhaps exceptionally well.

Chapter 8

Conclusions

 *T*hrough the course of analyses that we have taken in this work, the various ways that men and women can interpret each other's personality traits have become apparent. We have further investigated how such interpretations affect relations between men and women. Our study has revealed that the mechanisms of interpretation have changed over time in the Western world, and key psychological issues underlying the creation and maintenance of relationships are often neglected in the modern age. Let us review the key concepts we have covered.

Everyone at one point or another conceptualizes the honest ideal relationship, a mutually enhancing partnership which will provide fulfilment. In such a relationship, the idea of mutuality must predominate, where each person puts equal resources into serving goals of the other. From such a balanced arrangement, a vision of wholeness is expressed in the ideal family life, where there is security, growth, and advancement for the couple. No doubt, this is a worthy goal, and historically in European traditions such a relationship has been sanctioned and protected by the laws governing marriage. However, for those who do seek to reach the ideal, and refuse to accept the false, then the true nature of 'attraction' must be discerned. Although the perception of attractiveness is based on the evaluation of many attributes, it is usually personality that garners the most attention. Indeed, the world cannot understand the real person without interpreting the qualities of the 'persona', i.e., the public expression of an individual's mental components. Accordingly, the understanding of traits—the most intimate, distinctive aspects of a person—should be of critical importance in structuring a mutually respectful, enduring relationship.

Thus, throughout history, men and women have paid close attention to each other's opinions about various issues, especially those about relationships and family life. Indeed, all people contemplating marriage will evaluate a potential mate's various characteristics, and the courtship process has been a place where men and women could learn about each other's attitudes, opinions, beliefs, and habits. In certain social situations, the procedure to discover personality dimensions of someone else is not without difficulty, as personal attributes are often numerous and complex. In European cultures, the tendency has been for a man or woman to first assess the other person's opinions and attitudes, before obtaining their background traits, such as age, income, ethnicity, and family history. Asking about points of view and convictions is usually not considered impertinent, but enquiring about other personal connections and activities might be considered intrusive. Although such tactful manoeuvring might become tedious, it is, nonetheless, essential in maintaining an agreeable mutual discovery process.

At a certain point, each person would have enough information to form an estimation of the level of congruence between the various attributes. It is natural for one person to be attracted to another who has similar characteristics, as similarity makes for ease of communication, and increases trust because behaviour becomes more predictable. Similarities can be identified quickly and easily, and these could be the initial elements of attraction. However, although interpersonal differences might not be immediately attractive, they might often be considered a catalyst for the future development of both husband and wife. In traditional times (i.e., the era before c. 1800), European cultures understood that differences between husband and wife fostered an environment of mutual learning, growth, and maturing. Each person could learn from the other new ways of thinking and doing, and each person could also expect to depend on the other person for compensation in weakness. There could be a dovetailing of interests, a *complementarity*, which actually would strengthen the relationship, making it more fulfilling. Nonetheless, maturity, cooperation, good judgement, and guidance are required to reach this ideal of complementarity. This is why differences have always been further appraised in order to determine whether they were so considerable that the relationship might actually suffer because of them. The level of difference that would be regarded as 'unacceptable', although sometimes obvious, is often derived from a confluence of cultural, familial, and experiential factors. If the differences between the courting man and woman were not considered objectionable, then the possibility occurred that such divergences could be beneficial.

Living out the above model of family was relatively easier in traditional times, because this model incorporated *individualised* adjustments and expressions, allowing close affectional ties between people, both related and unrelated. An objective assessment of one's own needs and the social environment was encouraged, and no one had to rush into anything that was less then secure. There were, of course, cases where certain people were coerced into marital unions, but the ideal of marriage of family life was acknowledged by nearly everyone, and there was the *expectation* that the individual would do his best to implement this ideal (for the historical aspects, see Sporer 2010A).

Quite distinct from this ideal of the family, a new ideal of 'progress' developed during the 19th century. This ideal was thoroughgoing, and its advocates forcefully promulgated the concept that every generation should be 'better' than the previous one, there should be 'advancement' in every area of human endeavour, whether health, comfort, possessions, living space, or mental functioning. Human beings were now viewed, not as individuals, but as units: The average person was no longer a citizen and gentleman, he was a worker and consumer. Many believed that in this way, society could reach ever higher levels of material achievement through the new methods of social organisation; people now had to work in different ways, they had to move from their former homes, they had to learn new things.

Yet, the pressures from the outside induced many people to alter the way they dealt with each other. There were changes in who was considered 'eligible' for friendship, for the world had become more intimidating, it brought negative things from the outside into the home; most importantly, people did not know how these threats could be deflected, neutralised, converted, or defeated. There are advantages to having a large circle of acquaintances, but the changes in social relations in the 19th century made friendships with people outside the family more precarious. Many turned inward towards finding a new scheme, since too many enormous changes had already occurred in everyday life to be complacent about matrimony. The tradition of affection between men and

women continued, but the circle of friends shrank. People still felt
the need to marry, but the range of suitors was becoming smaller,
and since there were few social mechanisms for men and women
to socialise with each other, people often turned to family members
for friendship and also for marriage. In time, women could no
longer take up a sisterly relationship with a male who belonged
outside a two-degree limit, unless they could tolerate rumours
about immoral behaviour. From within the ranks of one's own
extended family could suitable friends be found, whose personalities were known by other family members, and who at the very
least could be bound from devolving into selfish behaviour by what
Victorians thought was the reflexive instinctual repulsion to taking
advantage of another family member. Hence, we see a large increase in the numbers of cousin marriage in the Western world,
which demonstrates this dynamic of a reduced social circle. There
was also a focus on the relationship between brother and sister,
and this served as a very acceptable and fulfilling alternative to
marriage.

Not only was courtship changing, but the various entities of the
Industrial age were encroaching on the family, causing a modification of its functioning. Since women were expected to run the
household, they were the ones most affected by these changes in
concepts of family. Women had marital and maternal 'duties' to
perform, such as to provide her husband with intimacy, raise children, and maintain a home. Moreover, in their position as 'chief'
of household affairs, they were expected to be 'experts' in raising
children, and in domestic matters. Indeed, now more than ever
they were expected to perform flawlessly in their role as making
their own 'assigned' contribution to the world. In fact, family roles

have been reconstituted, so that especially the feminine has been changed, with aspects of it being masculinised. Thus, on the one hand all women were expected to be prototypically 'feminine' by having children and raising them properly, but on the other hand, they had to take on 'masculine' traits, in order to work in the labour force. We can see that in the modern period, society became more complex, and greater sacrifices to the collective was expected of ordinary people. In the family sphere, this had special implications. Many women did not properly understand all the implications that attended to the emerging role of 'housewife'.

The latter half of the so-called Victorian era proved most interesting in regard to the process of equalising the sexes. Individual initiative, safeguarded as it was in the traditional period, was slowly being etiolated by the numerous demands of business and social functions which admitted little room for manoeuvre. The social climate of the Western world, dependent on economic functioning, produced social standards that demanded conformity to school, work, group, government rules, laws, regulations. A loss of individuality might have occurred in such an environment, but traditional concepts of humanitarianism were still present, and respect for these concepts stopped people from giving away their precious individuality.

In this milieu, where social obligations could only weakly be discerned in the blur of one set of concepts fading and another set emerging, it was inevitable that a new 'modern' set of standards would be established. Once these standards were put in place, using formal and informal means, then even before they meet, a man and woman can effectively predict the other person's attitudes on issues such as fertility, child-rearing, work, and household structure. Consequently, the widespread desire for predictability impelled a variety of social actors—from politicians, to educators, to scientists—to propagate a consistent set of simplifications to the domain of family. These actors attained the much coveted status of standard-setters because of their education, social position, group affiliation, and the confidence with which they espoused their beliefs. These authors of the new paradigm attempted to instigate a 'consciousness' amongst the peoples of the Western world that would make people feel obliged to marry, have children, and participate in the workforce, despite their fears.

Because of the complexity of gaining consensus amongst so many people, the new consciousness had to settle on one main issue, that of fertility. It was thought that by implementing limitations in family size, the goals of attaining greater household resources, proper indoctrination of children, and women participating in the labour force could all be achieved. Therefore, three successive standards were implemented. The first essentially sought to eliminate large families, of approximately 7 or more children; this standard did not advocate a particular size as 'ideal', but it did discourage high fertility. The second standard, somewhat more coherent than the first, distinctly encouraged having no more than three children. The third standard set the modern 'ideal' of the two child family. Hence, society began to interfere in the creation of marital relationships, more often in the negative sense, where social penalties might be incurred if there was too great a divergence from the 'norm'. These standards were ostensibly established in order to raise the family from poverty and lower class circumstances, but they also reduced the many different concepts of family structure that had existed in the traditional period.

Had they lived long enough, the social and political commentators in the 19th century who sought to implement a 'modernisation' of the family, would have seen their goals substantially met, for the simplifications to family structure did indeed reduce the costs of finding a marriage partner, through the narrowing of the variety and diversity of interpersonal experiences. The mentality established in the early 20th century was that marriage partners should be similar in traits from the beginning, as changes afterward, although possible to an extent, would be difficult. Such an approach, truly a radical departure from traditionalism, was justified on the basis of 'efficiency', that the 'cost' to society was would be reduced if all aspects of personality—tastes, preferences, values, even speech patterns—were regularised and standardised.

However, the 'experts' realised that not all differences could be eliminated in such a fashion. Economic and demographic factors have made many modern populations quite heterogenous, and it is likely that the average person will not easily find other people of similar background. The level of variability of opinion within a group makes a difference as to how easily someone will find a spouse that is acceptably similar. If there is enough time made for the search, then most people will find such a 'compatible' partner. But often the distractions of modern life, and the pressure to marry before 30, make this finding 'compatible' partners less likely for the majority of people.

Indeed, it is unlikely in most Western societies that such homology can be attained from the very beginning of a relationship. But there are also personal reasons that have brought about a reluctance to accept interpersonal differences. The modern economic structure has indirectly encouraged people to be self-centred, ready to relinquish the need for constructive dependence, and instead turning to exploitative tactics. The rigours of the workplace, as well as demographic changes that produce migration, isolation, and distancing from relatives, mean the many persons must attempt to find compensatory relationships, including a marriage partner, but through self-serving motives. The loss of traditional values has also resulted in less obligation to be flexible and cooperative, which leads to over-dependence on a spouse for support, but at the same time, to less cooperation. These actions do not improve relationships, but are likely to weaken and degrade them.

The changes we have been discussing are disturbing, not only because they constitute an unprecedented major break from the past, but because they directly and indirectly attack individualism. We must realise that the modern system of social relations betrays numerous weaknesses, and no sensible person would say that a new approach is not needed. Based on a consideration of the evidence, the first modification in the present paradigm should be the elimination of 'standards' of family type. No one should advocate a large family or small family as the 'right' way, for this is not in keeping with a European heritage that has put a premium on preserving individual thinking and initiative. Of course, European tradition has never tolerated foolishness, and everyone should choose, as best they can, a family type that is supportable and sustainable. What we are saying is that people should not only have the freedom to *choose* their family configuration without unnecessary social intrusion, but, even more importantly, they should be encouraged to take the opportunity to gain *complete knowledge* about the configurations that are derived from the carefully reasoned paradigms of their European ancestors. Western culture must accept again the idea that the members of their society should have the total liberty to contemplate various family types and select from among them as they see fit, with criticism occurring only if the choice was unreasonable and harmful to family or society.

If we are to find a way for Western culture to bring back the more prudent judgements of the traditional era, then it is likely to be most easily found in the 'homogenising' mechanisms. Migration and the demands of business and commerce have created a divergence of attitudes, with the result that long standing traditions and customs have been abandoned or relinquished. Many believed that the economic- and demographic-induced vagaries of culture and ethnicity had to be erased in order to provide men and women with a 'pool' of potential marriage partners, who were attractive by virtue of their mirror-like qualities. But this attempt did not work. Significant interpersonal differences still exist, and so certain social mechanisms have to be utilised to reduce disagreement and create a homogeneous set of opinions, not only for individuals, but an entire group. Now people often prefer that the range of attitudes and opinions be 'compressed' into simplistic conformity.

Attitudes and opinions can be modified through external agencies, and of these formal education is effective in bringing a greater chance of congruence, but surprisingly, higher education also can produce diversity in other areas. We earlier had analysed this situation from the perspective of the simple assimilation of information by the student. However, if there is a chance for positive complementarity to return to relationships, as it operated in traditional family configurations, then we must take into account the dynamics that link the educational institution, the teachers who represent them, and the student's background, values, concepts, and goals.

The higher education environment invariably contains a multi-
tude of hypotheses of general behaviour that students must at least
acknowledge; these theories sometimes introduce new concepts,
and sometimes they clash with or reinforce existing concepts. Professors, as well as textbooks, can put forward apparent principles
on a wide variety of areas, some of which deal, albeit indirectly,
with marriage. We see evidence that indicates that students seem
to accept more willingly, possibly out of a *sense of social obligation,*
theories related to the interrelationship of various social types, but
they treat with more scepticism issues that require personal interpretation, such as the social importance of savings, work experience, and education. These aspects clearly can be associated with
marriage, as the educational environment can make opinions about
life before marriage more homogeneous. Hence, the educational
system succeeds in gaining consensus in areas such as whether one
should marry; whether one's relations with friends and parents
after marriage are improved; whether one should marry someone
who is physically unattractive; whether one should marry someone
of a different race; whether one should marry someone with children. If it were stressed that the goal in attending college was the
development of mental processes and ascertaining verified facts,
and not necessarily ingesting theories, then it is likely many people
would become more individualised in their thinking again.

Further, the dynamics of the group are strong in a college setting. This is implied in the Latin term *collegium,* which means a
society where power and authority are vested equally in all members. This creates the impression that, since all students are 'peers'
gathered together in one distinct rank, above that of common
society, they should all think alike. Students may feel that they are

obliged to carry similar opinions, since this is what it means to be 'college-educated'. Consequently, the emphasis on group affiliation should be minimised, and instead, individualised reasoning processes should be promoted.

At the beginning of this work, we stated the philosophers have considered the factors that make for the ideal relationship. It is sad to think that many imposters have taken the place of geniuses in order to promulgate concepts that harm marriages, and make it difficult for people to reconcile those very intelligent differences between them that could lead to a better life. There is always the capacity to learn, but modern man has been reduced to the status of near-moron by the supposed guardians of culture, who, regrettably, have turned out to be self-serving charlatans.

Economic factors continue to have a dominant role in modern life, where all of society appears to be a slave to the new ideal of 'progress'. Those ancient traditions that prevailed in Europe were modified or relinquished because they gave people too much impetus to be 'different' from the average, to believe in 'extraordinary' things. Further research needs to carried out into the reasons why traditionally some couples wanted large families, others wanted smaller ones, and still other couples wanted no children. Our ancestors understood the motivations that went into each configuration, and society found it necessary to accommodate itself to individual plans. In modern society, however, it is the individual who must accommodate himself to social forces, especially relating to the industrial business complex. The average person has become afraid to invite other people to learn about private matters; social relations have become more stiff and formal, everything is treated in a 'business-like' manner, with little room for genuine sharing of emotions and feelings. External demands on time and affiliation emanating from the modern economy are responsible for the decreasing emphasis on personal sacrifice and the willingness to change, with a concomitant fostering of views that assure group solidarity.

In fact, we have seen that the modern age has imposed unrealistic expectations on marital relationships. A clash between 'traditional' and 'modern' has taken place. Social trends since the beginning of the Industrial Age have attempted to impair or remove those mechanisms that assist the married couple to properly utilise personality attributes. Contemporary culture even casts aspersions on the very idea of 'deepening their relationship'. The modern age no longer looks at individuals as potentially powerful sources of knowledge and wisdom, but merely as economic 'units of production', who are 'good' only as long as they obey commands from those in authority.

Congruence in habits and opinions, in order to bring about ease of relationship, is stressed in all cultures as facilitating social interaction, but this concept in the modern world has taken on a *determining* aspect, meaning that convergence of opinion is essential. For many people, if congruence cannot be found, then the relationship cannot be maintained. If two people marry, even with the best 'intentions', and then discover that their differences are too great, in that they cause friction that cannot be overcome, then divorce must seriously be considered. The modern belief is that time will not increase similarity between husband and wife, and thus after several years of difficulties, the marriage will end because the couple were never 'compatible'. The prevalence of divorce indicates that people are often wrong in their judgements of other people, even of those whom they supposedly know intimately, and it is likely that self-deception is prevalent in the Western population.

Notwithstanding these difficulties, the intelligent and astute individual should have no fear of differences. Variations in attitudes between two persons can be enriching and enlightening, as long as they totally secure in their agreement on fundamental issues. Of course, we are not advocating that the individual accept *all* ideas that are unlike his own, for traits must be judged on their moral, ethical, and intellectual merits. Whatever characteristics are based on selfishness, stupidity, greed, should be rejected, and indeed, such traits would be poison in any relationship. However, positive personal attitudes, whether towards marriage, household, child-rearing, employment, etc, can be reconciled very confidently within the sturdy confines of a loving, respectful relationship founded on a clear, consistent conceptualisation of the boundaries of behaviour. There would be no embarrassment, no repulsion, no apprehension, no recriminations in such a relationship. Dissimilarity does not imply disagreement. Attitudinal differences, based as they are on the components of experience, history, and observation, can be the conduit of relevant and surprisingly useful information. Most importantly, the acceptance of differences between a man and woman, in the appropriate circumstances, builds strong bonds that endure, and that no one can sever.

Notes

1   Although a very large country rooted in pre-modern traditions has many variants in regard to mate selection, it would appear that at least in some cultures in India stress that individuals select potential mates, but with parental approval. Choosing a mate involves careful analysis of personality and socio-cultural attributes, including personal income, religion and caste, whereas occupation is not important. However, these considerations do not seem to be as meaningful among Indian immigrants to America (Sharma & Rajlakshmi 1979; Siddiqi & Reeves 1986). Assortative mating in the more economically modern, but still socially traditional Orkney Islands included considerations of kinship, demographic, social and geographic factors (Brennan & Dyke 1980). Around the world, the selection and final approval of a mate are becoming matters increasingly in the hands of the individual; because of this, probably more people will marry late, and more will not marry at all (Murstein 1980). The most 'advanced' form of mate selection uses computers. For example, 1000 pieces of information (in 108 categories) are taken from each person, compared to ideals set forth by the individual, and then compared to an ideal put forward by a marriage counsellor. The computer can predict which areas are most likely to be most rewarding and which areas are most troublesome (Smith & Debenham 1979). Automatic

matching efforts, whether ancient or modern, where people are paired off by simple rules, do not by themselves
seem to yield lower divorce rates nor happier marriages,
in spite of the millions using such procedures and services.
It appears that only when the individual considering marriage and the matchmaker are from a relatively *homogeneous cultural background* does an 'expert system' work.

2   It is not surprising that many girls take on masculine
characteristics and interests in order to ease the transition
from same-sex friendship to opposite-sex friendship, and
on to opposite-sex romance. Such disguises often bring
difficulty with boyfriends later on when the need for
complementarity arises.

3   Scanzoni 1968.

4   Heer 1974. Often the word homology refers to any similarity that is the result of common origin. In this work, we
are not using it explicitly as such, although frequently
people who do have very similar attitudes and behaviours
tend to come from the same background, racial group, or
region.

5   Christensen & Barber 1967; Bumpass & Sweet 1972.

6   Howard, et al. 1989.

7   Bentler & Newcomb 1978; Chadwick & Heaton 1992, p 84.
We should not make the mistake of overgeneralising in
these matters, however. The role of personality differences
in relationships can be perceived socially in various ways,

depending on a community's history, ethnic composition, and culture.

8   Bainbridge & Stark 1981.

9   Hansen & Hicks 1980.

10 The desire for, and approval of, homology between married couples is not new. Writers, divines, and moralists endorsed similarity in religious belief, age, economic position and social background as early as the 16th century (Ozment 1983, p. 59).

11 Tambs & Moum 1992.

12 Argyle et al. 1985.

13 The survey was broken down by education and sex in Chadwick & Heaton (1992, pp 22-47). We cite only those answers where there is a clear change in the diversity of opinion due to educational attainment.

14 U.S. Department of Commerce 1985, Table 8, p 154.

15 One could reasonably argue that a difference of only one position on the scale might not be significant. For example, on the issue of saving money before marriage, a husband holds a position of 7 (very important) and his wife holds a position of 6 (quite important). Is there that much difference between the two positions that would lead to a clash? It is not so much the absolute difference between two positions, as it is the *degrees of certainty relative to the ends of the scale*. The fact that the largest percentages tend

to fall on positions 1, 4, or 7 (especially for the poorly educated) indicates the ideological importance of these positions. Falling on one of these pivotal steps in the scale might be seen as a 'declaration', with even the smallest deviance a disavowal. Clearly, if a man is very adamant about an issue (say holding a position 1 or 7), he might find it irritating when someone else is only one step away. He might feel similarly if he is firmly in the centre (at 4), and someone else is only at 3 or 5.

16   In this way, people will quickly know within a particular social context where someone stands even before meeting them, facilitating the socialising and marriage process. If the majority have easy access to people who share their views, and are not willing to date people who differ from their views, then the minority must set up an 'underground' to effectively meet others who share their views, and who are as unconventional in beliefs as they are. The college environment both creates a convergence of opinion, as well as provides a venue for those who diverge from this consensus.

17   Rankin & Maneker 1987; comparisons are for couples who have divorced.

18   Jung 1968, p 20.

19   One could argue that since they have low income, women in this position could not leave the marriage, since they could not support themselves. This might be specious reasoning, as present income does not guarantee future

earnings potential, the ease of finding employment, or competence at work. A married woman who works only part-time could, after a divorce, go into full-time employment and earn an income that secures an autonomous lifestyle.

20   'To my feeling, this deadness to the history which has prepared half our world for us, this inability to find interest in any form of life that is not clad in the same coattails and flounces as our own lies very close to the worst kind of irreligion. The best that can be said of it is, that it is a sign of the intellectual narrowness—in plain English, the stupidity, which is still the average mark of our culture.' George Eliot (pen name of Marian Evans); (quoted from Kermode & Kermode 1995, p 346).

21   Vera et al. 1990.

22   People today are widely viewed as prisoners of their genes, reacting, especially in the deviant sense, to supposedly irrepressible urges, such as drinking, stealing, using drugs, sexual promiscuity, and violence. The ongoing effort to prove the physical basis for much of human behaviour is quite conspicuously a major goal in the behavioural sciences.

23   Hajnal 1983.

24   Veevers 1984.

25   Vera et al. 1990.

26   Basavarajappa et al. 1988, Canadian data.

27   If the idea of 'eternal youth' becomes fixed in society, then
      in the near future men and women will not be very differ-
      ent from each other, even when both are older, because
      an adult will not be expected to give up many of his or her
      childhood interests or attitudes. Women will still be able
      to behave in a fairly 'tomboyish' way. Young and old
      should not be very different, and the tendency for older
      men to marry younger women might then not be as preva-
      lent. Despite this increased similitude between youth and
      adult personalities, we should bear in mind that there will
      still be a distinction between the *obligations* of the married
      lifestyle and those of the single lifestyle.

28   Archer 1984.

29   Peres & Meivar 1986; the study used sample of classifieds
      in Israeli newspapers.

30   Hahn 1983.

31   In relation to films and the independence ethos, one de-
      fines and elucidates the masculine more easily and use-
      fully, with the feminine left in some ambiguity. A critical
      part of the feminine is to express doubt, to raise objections
      to bold (ordinarily masculine) plans. The feminine can be
      characterised by caution, that is, a belief that a venture
      may not succeed in reaching its goal. Perhaps because of
      the female tendency to focus on maintenance and local
      control, women can be indecisive and passive when it

comes to social matters. On the other hand, masculinity typically involves clear processes and methods, new ventures, and original concepts. The coming together of a 'sex-typed' man and woman can produce interesting results. Men in such a situation see the *absence* of mental and physical energy as 'feminine', and so a counterpart to their own decisiveness. This might make the male-female relationship far more attractive to a man than a same-sex friendship, because there is the opportunity his unique abilities to be appreciated. Further, a woman can be the place where he projects all that he finds uncertain, equivocal or enigmatic, thus removing these features from his own character. Women end up being the 'injured innocent', giving men the role of a 'knight', a guardian and leader ready to endure the failings of his companion (Jung 1959/68, paras. 169, 183). After a loss or disappointment, husbands might potentially blame their wives for being too timid and not taking chances, when in fact it might primarily be the husband's fault.

32 Atienza Hernández 1989.

33 Armstrong 1986. Contemporaries noted the common attitude of focussing attention on pleasure and materialism. Young people became much more independent-minded, and were considered to be undisciplined and anti-authoritarian. Patterns of courtship and sexual activity changed also. These observations correspond well to the evidence provided by social statistics where available (Shorter & Schmalfuss 1972).

34 For an interesting foretaste of feminism and the break-
    down in relations between the sexes, see the exchange of
    letters between Abigail and John Adams, (Kermode &
    Kermode 1995, letters 85 and 86), wherein Abigail entreats
    here husband to pass laws that curtail the power of Man,
    who is 'Naturally Tyrannical', and to use the power given
    to men for the women's 'happiness'. John laughs off such
    suggestions, but says that the 'Masculine systems' that give
    men power are never used in full force, because in reality
    'We [men] are the subjects' of women.' This is a common
    theme of the 'Enlightenment' era, where men deflect dis-
    cussions about the loss of chivalry and the precarious,
    uncertain position of women, by resorting to flattery, spe-
    cifically, professing a constitutional weakness for the
    Fairer Sex. It evades the issue of whether there is any kind
    of real superiority, in general or in precise areas, of the
    male over the female. Men must convey convincing rea-
    sons why a dominant role should be assigned to them, and
    why women should not fear the possibility that this au-
    thority will be exceeded. It is understandable that women
    are reluctant to say that their fears have been allayed,
    when the only thing standing between civil and uncivil
    use of power is a pretty face, or a charming manner.

35 Anderson 1986.

36 Shorter 1987.

37 Quote from *A Woman of No Importance* (1893).

38 For a description of these changes see Hawes 1985.

39 Hawes 1985, p 57.

40 Quotes taken from Hawes 1985.

41 Wrigley 1987, Fig. 10.5, p 258. When the two age groups are combined, there is less of a variation in fertility.

42 See for example American data in U.S. Bureau of the Census, 1975, Table B Columns 42–48, which shows, by modern standards, an amazing diversity in household types.

43 U.S. Bureau of the Census, 1975, Table B, Columns 42–48; U.S. Bureau of the Census, 1989, Table 101.

44 Chadwick & Heaton, 1992, p 111, Table D1-7, p 113, Table D1-9.

45 See U.S. Bureau of the Census, 1975, Table D, Column 60.

46 Just as decisions about family size varied from family to family, they probably varied from community to community, and region to region. If one could look across the cultural map of any nation, one would see a hodge-podge of practises and tendencies which reflected the traditions, exigencies, and innate temperament of the people. Since we rarely have anything resembling a complete set of cultural ideas for a community, let alone a region, scholars often resort to using language as a marker for culture; and where culture changes, so does language.

Even though France is renowned for its centralised government, a vast assortment of dialects and languages existed in the nation well into the 20th century. There were many who spoke no French, or spoke it badly, but nonetheless they believed French should be used for solemn occasions, for higher culture, and for sermons. The government encouraged the use of French as the exclusive language for all social strata, using the school system as its main agent. Older terms were either abandoned, or remained as names for certain common objects. Some peasants had difficulty making the adjustment because there were sometimes no words in French that were comparable to ones in their own dialect or language (Weber 1976, 67-94). The extensibility of the local language reflects other aspects of culture; one could use French when necessary, and another language when it suited the individual and the situation. The homogenisation of France was a necessity, if the country was to prosper (communications is critical in the development of any modern economy), but at the same time the people lost the ability to speak effectively, since the words that arose from a culture close to their hearts and minds were no more. The new language was instrumental, just as was the common national culture, but the old language and old ways which could preserve many nuances of attitudes, behaviours, and utilisation, were still useful in a human sense.

One wonders if the current lack of precision in vernacular speech, in countries such as America, might not be due to this imposition of a common dialect, leaving people who vary from the average temperament and experience without convenient words. In the same way that words and expressions give us an easy way to convey our desires, so too do cultural ideas, through maxims, legends, and events taken from previous generations. Hence, *the loss of diversity in speech parallels the homogenisation of culture.* The same that was said about language can be said about culture: People search for precise cultural answers to their personal difficulties, but are only offered rough and clumsy generic solutions. It is a paradox to say that modern people usually find satisfactory ways of doing most things, but are still frustrated by the inability of the common culture to give them the information and reassurance needed to reach their personal goals.

47 West & Morgan 1987; they also mention better birth control, although this is largely a function of the other two.

References

Anderson NF, 1986, Cousin marriage in Victorian England, *Journal of Family History*, 11(3), 285-301.

Archer J., 1984, Gender roles as developmental pathways, *British Journal of Social Psychology*, 23(3), 245-256.

Argyle M., Henderson M., Furnham A., 1985, The rules of social relationships, *The British Journal of Social Psychology*, Jun 24(2), 125-139.

Armstrong N., 1986, History in the house of culture: Social disorder and domestic fiction in early Victorian England, *Poetics Today*, 7(4), 641-671.

Atienza Hernández I., 1989, [Women and ideology: An emic vision of the role of the aristocratic woman in the seventeenth century], *Revista Internacional de Sociología*, 47(3), 317-337.

Bainbridge W.S., Stark R., 1981, Friendship, religion, and the occult: A network study, *Review of Religious Research*, Jun 22(4), 313-327.

Basavarajappa K.G., Norris MJ, Halli SS, 1988, Spouse selection in Canada, 1921-78: An examination by age, sex, and religion, *Journal of Biosocial Science*, Spr 20(2), 211-223.

Bentler P.M., Newcomb M.D., 1978, Longitudinal study of marital success and failure, *Journal of Consulting and Clinical Psychology*, 46, 1053-1070.

Brennan E.R., Dyke B, 1980, Assortative mate choice and mating opportunity on Sanday, Orkney Islands, *Social Biology*, Fal 27(3), 199-210.

Bumpass L.L., Sweet J.A., 1972, Differentials in marital instability: 1972, *American Sociological Review*, 37, 754-767.

Chadwick B.A., Heaton T.B., 1992, eds, *Statistical Handbook on the American Family*, Oryx Press, Phoenix.

Christensen H. T., Barber K.E., 1967, Interfaith versus intrafaith marriage in Indiana, *Journal of Marriage and the Family*, 29, 461-149.

Hahn A., 1983, [The fiction of consensus in small groups: The example of new marriages], *Kölner Zeitschrift für Soziologie und Sozialpsychologie*, Supl 25, 210-232.

Hajnal J., 1983, Two kinds of pre-industrial household formation system, in *Family Forms in Historic Europe*, R. Wall, J. Robin, P. Laslett, eds., 1983, Cambridge University Press, Cambridge.

Hansen S.L., Hicks M.W., 1980, Sex role attitudes and perceived dating-mating choices of youth, *Adolescence*, Spr 15(57), 83-90.

Hawes J.M., 1985, The strange history of female adolescence in the United States, *The Journal of Psychohistory*, Sum 13(1), 51-63.

Heer D.M., 1974, The prevalence of black-white marriage in the United States, 1960 and 1970, *Journal of Marriage and the Family*, 36, 246-258.

Howard J.A., Blumstein P., Schwartz P., 1989, Homogamy in intimate relationships: Why birds of a feathers flock together, paper presented at 84th annual meeting of the American Sociological Association.

Jung C.G., 1959/68, 'Psychological aspects of the mother archetype' (1939/54), in *The Archetypes and the Collective Unconscious*, Princeton University Press, Princeton, New Jersey.

Jung C.G., 1968, *Analytical Psychology: Its Theory and Practice: The Tavistock Lectures*, (1935), London and New York.

Kermode F., Kermode, A., 1995, *The Oxford Book of Letters*, Oxford University, Oxford.

Murstein B.I., 1980, Mate selection in the 1980s, *Journal of Marriage and the Family*, Nov 42(4), 777-792.

Ozment S., 1983, *When Fathers Ruled: Family Life in Reformation Europe*, Harvard University Press, Cambridge.

Peres Y., Meivar H., 1986, Self-presentation during courtship: A content analysis of classified advertisements in Israel, *Journal of Comparative Family Studies*, Spr 17(1), 19-31.

Rankin R.P., Maneker JS, 1987, Correlates of marital duration and black-white intermarriage in California, *Journal of Divorce*, Win 11(2), 51-67.

Scanzoni J., 1968, A social system analysis of dissolved and exiting marriages, *Journal of Marriage and the Family*, 30, 451-461.

Sharma A., Rajlakshmi S., 1979, Opinions of married couples regarding the selection of the marriage partner: A study of couples residing in Baroda, *Sociological Bulletin*, Mar-Sep 28(1-2), 71-82.

Shorter E, 1987, The first great increase in anorexia nervosa, *Journal of Social History*, Fall, 69-96.

Shorter E., Schmalfuss A., 1972, 'La Vie Intime'—Contributions to its history on the example of cultural change in the Bavarian lower classes in the 19th century, *Kolner Zeitschrift für Soziologie und Sozialpsychologie*, 16, Suppl, 530-549.

Siddiqi M.U., Reeves E.Y., 1986, A comparative study of mate selection criteria among Indians in India and the United States, *International Journal of Comparative Sociology*, 27(3-4), 226-233.

Smith G.W., Debenham J.D., 1979, Computer automated marriage analysis, *The American Journal of Family Therapy*, Spr 7(1), 16-31.

Sporer, P.D., 2010A, *Liberating Love*, Quenstedt Press, Chester.

Sporer, P.D., 2010B, *The Dimensions of Companionship*, Quenstedt Press, Chester.

Sporer, P.D., 2010C, *The Concept of Family*, Quenstedt Press, Chester.

Tambs K., Moum T., 1992, No large convergence during marriage for health, lifestyle, and personality in a large sample of Norwegian spouses, *Journal of Marriage and the Family*, 54(4), 957-971.

U.S. Bureau of the Census, 1975, *Historical Statistics of the United States, Colonial Times to 1970, Parts 1 and 2*, Washington, DC.

U.S. Bureau of the Census, 1989, *Statistical Abstract of the United States*, 1989, (109th edition) Washington, DC.

U.S. Department of Commerce, 1985, *1980 Census of the Population*, Volume 2 Subject Reports, Marital Characteristics, U.S. Government Printing Office, Washington, DC.

Veevers J.E., 1984, Age-discrepant marriages: cross-national comparisons of Canadian-American trends, *Social Biology*, Spr-Sum 31(1-2), 18-27.

Vera H., Berardo F.M., Vandiver J.S., 1990, Age irrelevancy in society: The test of mate selection, *Journal of Aging Studies*, Spr 4(1), 81-95.

Weber E., 1976, *Peasants into Frenchmen, The Modernization of Rural France, 1870-1914,* Stanford University Press, Stanford, California.

West K.K., Morgan L.A., 1987, Public perceptions of the ideal number of children for contemporary families, *Population and Environment Behavioral and Social Ideas,* Fal 9(3), 160-172.

Wrigley E.A., 1987, *People, Cities and Wealth,* Basil Blackwell, Oxford.

Index

abandonment, 4, 46

absolute, 21, 29

abstract, 17, 19, 28, 83

academic, 16, 26, 88

accommodate, 37, 39, 101

accomplishments, 26, 78

account, 56, 70, 99

actors, 96

admired traits, 10

adulthood, 2, 45, 71, 76, 77

advanced, 5, 27, 46, 80

advantage, 10, 94

affection, 1, 40, 61, 64, 66, 67, 71, 72, 76, 80, 87, 93

age of 18, 76

agreement, 9, 11, 17, 19, 25–27, 31, 32, 34, 35, 60, 103

alter, 22, 34, 39, 78, 93

anorexia nervosa, 76, 77

arguments, 22, 48, 77

arise, 19, 60, 88

arrangements, 46, 64, 90

assertiveness, 11, 55

assimilation, 99

attempt, 3, 7, 18, 38, 41, 71, 73, 85, 98, 99

attention, 44, 61, 66, 78, 84, 91

attitudes, 2, 5–7, 12, 13, 17, 19, 28, 30, 32, 33, 37, 41, 47, 49, 51, 52, 54, 60, 61, 68, 75, 85, 87, 88, 91, 95, 99, 103

attraction, 5, 15, 32, 66, 70, 72, 92

attractive, 49, 50, 92, 99

attributes, 1, 4, 12, 13, 16, 26, 48, 49, 51, 52, 54, 55, 63, 91, 102

authority, 21, 44, 62, 65, 73, 80, 88, 100, 102

autonomy, 26, 45, 65

background, 6–8, 10–13, 16, 19, 26, 34, 35, 37, 38, 48, 69, 72, 74, 89, 91, 97, 99

balance, 6, 36, 37, 53, 55, 86

basis, 9, 13, 21, 72, 97

belief, 4, 5, 15, 17, 22, 27, 32, 33, 39, 42, 49, 51, 102

benefit, 3, 20, 36

birth. *See* fertility

bond, 10, 31, 76, 103

boundaries, 3, 43, 103

brother. *See* family

build, 4, 11, 16, 46, 48

capacity, 59, 101

caring, 39, 59, 64, 65, 79

career, 6, 8, 26, 27, 68, 79;
employment, 16, 28, 36, 40,
60, 62, 68, 103; job, 23, 24,
27, 28, 40, 52; work, 4, 9,
14, 18, 28, 33, 34, 36, 44, 47,
48, 51–53, 66, 69, 77–79, 83,
85, 88, 89, 90, 93, 95,
99–101. *See also* financial
issues

celibacy. See pre-marital relations

century, 48, 50, 55, 64, 67, 69,
70, 72, 74, 75, 77, 86, 89, 93,
97

challenges, 28, 32, 37, 49, 55,
73, 78, 85, 87

character, 12, 15–17

characteristics: assertiveness,
11; chastity, 64; curiosity,
15; deceit, 60, 103; foolishness, 98; honesty, 40, 63;
integrity, 40; intelligence,
63, 89; traits, 4–6, 8–12,
14–16, 37, 49–51, 56, 63, 70,

90, 91, 95, 97, 103; virtue, 1,
33, 36, 40, 45, 63, 67, 99;
wisdom, 3, 39, 73, 86, 102

chastity, 64

childhood, 1, 44, 45, 54, 71, 77

children. *See* family

circumstances, 37, 39, 43, 55,
65, 85, 96, 103

citizen, 37, 93

class. *See* status

climate, 68, 95

coincidence, 8, 48

collective, 6, 85, 95

collective origins, 42

commerce, 61, 65, 99

commitment, 8, 78

communication, 6, 91

community, 39, 85

companionship, 1, 9, 12, 26

compassion, 1, 44, 63

competence, 46

competition, 58

complementary, 11

compromise, 39, 40

concept, 2, 3, 8, 28, 49, 57, 61,
62, 64, 65, 69, 82, 93, 102

concern, 1, 16, 57, 88

confidence, 96

conflict, 8, 27, 32

congruence, 16, 18, 21, 60, 91, 99, 102

conscientiously, 59, 85

constructive, 14, 28, 43, 44, 57, 58, 71, 98

contentment, 86

context, 8, 9, 30, 47, 65, 86, 91

convention, 32, 89

convergence, 17, 34, 102

cooperation, 1, 11, 37, 43, 46, 75, 92, 98

correlations, 13, 14

counterparts, 28

couple (two people), 10, 16–19, 22, 31, 33, 35, 37–39, 48, 51, 57, 59, 102

courtship. *See* pre-marital relations

creation, 4, 33, 90, 96

critical, 2, 10, 16, 17, 19, 20, 36, 48, 55, 68, 74, 79, 81, 84, 91

criticism, 56, 99

cultivating productive citizens, 37

customs, 6, 99

dating. *See* pre-marital relations

deception, 60, 103

defective, 4, 12, 41

demographic, 38, 82, 84, 87, 97–99

depth, 6, 7, 10, 11, 16, 31, 57, 58, 63, 72

desire, 1–3, 6, 9, 11, 20, 30, 46, 52, 55, 56, 70–72, 76, 77, 96

desire for autonomy, 45

details, 16, 62

development, 2, 3, 32, 51, 60, 61, 69, 82, 92, 100

differences, 4, 42, 53, 56, 58, 92, 97

difficulty, 58, 80, 91

diligence, 11, 89

disappointment, 19

discipline, 63

discussions, 47, 48, 52, 61, 71, 76

disposition, 9, 56

distance, 5, 10, 17, 43

divisions, 32, 84

divorce. *See* marriage

doctors, 71, 77, 78

domain, 10, 44, 54, 56, 76, 80, 96

domestic. *See* household

dovetailing, 10, 31, 92

drug use, 65, 81

early marriage. *See* marriage
economy, 40, 61, 74, 102
education and learning: classroom, 17, 21; colleges, 17, 21, 22, 26, 28, 30, 32, 33, 85, 100; general, 8, 13, 15, 20, 21–24, 26, 27, 31–34, 35–37, 44, 46, 48, 60, 62, 78, 79, 84, 85, 89, 92, 96, 99, 100; professors, 100; schooling, 27, 36; schools, 9, 26, 78, 95; students, 21, 85, 99, 100; teachers, 99; universities, 85
efficiency, 66, 86
embodied, 35, 64
emotion: anger, 33; general aspects, 14, 70, 102; embarrassment, 103; fear, 40, 67, 68, 75, 103; happiness, 76, 83, 87; shyness, 48
emotional intimacy: affection, 1, 40, 61, 64, 66, 67, 71, 72, 76, 80, 87, 93; compassion, 1, 44, 63; intimacy, 58, 72, 76, 94; intimate, 2, 4, 5, 8, 11, 13, 17, 19, 59, 70, 72, 73,

91; romance, 7, 9, 69. *See also* virtue
employment. *See* career
encourage, 5, 21, 43, 47, 85
enterprise, 69, 78
entertainment, 53, 85
entrustment, 39
equality, 8, 28, 32, 45, 62, 76
equality in attitudes, 12
era, 61, 79, 92, 95, 99
essential, 15, 43, 52, 72, 91, 102
ethos, 46, 48
Eugenics, 48, 70
Europe and Europeans: Britain, 81; France, 76; general, 2–4, 40, 43, 44, 46, 68, 87, 90–92, 98, 101; Switzerland, 77
examination, 49, 75, 84
existence, 19, 58
exploitation, 67, 98
expression, 1, 5, 64, 72, 80
extent, 18, 19, 34, 36, 37, 43, 50, 58, 68, 77, 83, 97
external, 16, 37, 55, 61, 75, 99, 102
extraordinary, 62, 87

failure, 3, 86

family: brothers, 72, 94; children, 1, 2, 24, 26, 32, 33, 36, 42, 44, 54, 59, 60, 62, 64–68, 71, 72, 75–79, 81–84, 86, 88, 89, 94–96, 100, 101, 103; cousins, 68–72, 94; fathers, 62, 71; general aspects, 1, 3, 4, 7, 19, 36, 38, 39, 43, 44, 58, 60–64, 66–71, 73, 74–76, 78, 80–82, 84–88, 90–99; large, 82, 84, 96, 101; mothers, 62, 75, 78, 79, 84; parents, 1, 2, 11, 23, 26, 47, 53, 69, 71, 100; siblings, 1, 62, 68, 69, 72; sisters, 72, 94; small, 82, 98

fantasy, 42, 71

fathers. *See* family

fear. *See* emotion

feeling, 28, 44

feminine, 54, 55, 62, 63, 79, 95

fertility, 81–84, 88, 95, 96
    births, 52, 73, 79, 81–83
    general, 81–84, 88, 95, 96
    illegitimacy, 65, 66

financial issues: employment, 16, 23, 24, 27, 28, 36, 40, 52, 60, 62, 68, 103; general, 38, 59, 84, income, 16, 26, 45, 91, industrial age, 77, 80, 87, 89, 94, 102; industrialism, 36, 40, 61, 65, 68, 74, 77, 80, 85, 87, 89, 94, 101, 102; inheritance, 48, 61; money, 23, 27, 38, 65; poverty, 41, 96; savings, 23, 27, 33, 34, 100; wealth, 21, 69

flexibility, 40

food, 9, 44, 45

formal education. *See* education and learning

frame of mind, 39

fraud, 65

freedom, 23, 27, 28, 36, 61, 75, 79, 84, 98, 99

friction, 15, 18, 19, 34, 102

friends, 7, 22, 26, 36, 68, 73, 94, 100

friendship, 2, 3, 5, 7–9, 17, 19, 23, 29, 31, 68, 93, 94

frustration, 18, 33, 60

fulfilment, 1, 3, 11, 57, 61, 67, 75, 79, 90

fundamental, 5, 14, 19, 30, 32, 48, 56, 84, 103

future. *See* history

gender, 5

generations, 37, 39, 42, 51, 75, 77, 86

genetics, 14, 15, 48, 70

genuine, 3, 35, 57, 63, 77, 101

God, 65

government and politics: general, 13, 60, 65, 84, 88, 95, 97; institutions, 21, 34; nation, 46, 49, 50, 84; nationalist, 40; politicians, 96; revolution, 40, 47, 65, 68, 87

gratification, 1, 5, 30, 61, 66

group dynamics: association, 30; community, 39, 85; conventions, 89; criticism, 2, 10, 16, 17, 19, 20, 36, 48, 55, 56, 68, 74, 79, 81, 84, 91, 99; friendship, 2, 3, 5, 7–9, 17, 19, 22, 23, 26, 29, 31, 36, 68, 73, 93, 94, 100; general, 8, 9, 14, 16, 18, 29–32, 40, 48, 51–53, 55, 59, 62, 65–67, 81, 84, 95–97, 99–102; group solidarity, 102; group-orientated, 40; heterology, 4, 5, 10–12, 15, 27, 28, 57; homology, 4–8, 11, 12, 13–15, 19, 39, 49–51, 55, 60, 68, 73,

80, 82, 97; progress, 69; rules, 16, 17, 75, 80, 81, 86, 95; threats, 66, 93. *See also* traditional

happiness. *See* emotion

harmony, 8, 26, 35–37, 40, 41, 44, 46

health issues, 47, 48, 93

helplessness, 44

heterology. *See* traits

heterophily. *See* traits

historical, 62, 93

history: 19th century, 67, 69, 70, 72, 74, 75, 77, 89, 93, 97; 20th century, 48, 50, 55, 64, 74, 77, 86, 97; ancient, 101; culture, 9, 19, 38, 39, 42, 44, 45, 58, 61, 63, 80, 84, 87, 98, 99, 101, 102; early modern, 50, 81; future, 1, 16, 35, 64, 88, 92; general, 2, 11, 33, 38, 39, 42, 69, 70, 75, 78, 91, 103; Middle Ages, 50; Victorian, 69, 95

hobbies, 16

home, 27, 30, 36, 47, 61, 63, 65, 71, 81–83, 93, 94

homology. *See* traits

homophily. *See* traits

honesty, 40, 63, 90

household, 30, 31, 33, 38, 39, 44, 45, 47, 59, 60, 62, 64–66, 71, 78, 80, 81, 85, 86, 88, 94–96, 103; domesticity, 44, 64, 67, 76–79, 94; expenses, 9, 44, 45; large size, 82, 96

human, 1–3, 7, 15, 19, 42, 47, 48, 58, 69, 71, 72, 93

humanitarianism, 42, 95

husband. *See* marriage

idea, 7, 39, 43, 47, 48, 59, 60, 76, 79, 81, 83, 88, 90, 99, 102

ideals: general, 1, 3, 4, 11, 12, 18, 41, 42, 48, 61, 63–67, 74, 76, 79, 80, 82–84, 90, 92, 93, 101; high standard, 37, 67; ideal family, 82, 90; ideal marriage, 42, 84; ideal of love, 3, 11, 12, 42; ideal woman, 65

ideological positions, 8

illegitimacy, 65

image, 7, 89

immature, 2, 44, 58

improvement, 10, 15, 44

income. *See* financial issues

independence, 13, 27, 40, 46, 67, 74, 79, 84, 88

independence ethos, 46

individual, 1, 6, 10, 13–15, 20, 27, 30, 38–44, 56, 61, 72, 74, 75, 77, 78, 86, 88, 89, 91, 93, 95, 98, 101, 103

individualism, 98

individuality, 43, 59, 81, 87, 95

Industrial Age, 77, 80, 87, 89, 94, 102

inflexibility, 40

inherent, 62

inheritance. *See* financial issue

innate, 14, 15, 79, 91

inspiration, 66

instability, 60, 81

instinctual, 7, 14, 70, 72, 73, 94

institutions, 21, 34, 58, 62, 66, 99

intelligence, 63, 89

interpretation, 34, 90, 100

intimacy. *See* emotional intimacy

isolation, 43, 98

join, 1, 33, 67

judgements, 92, 99, 102

judgments, 13, 16

justified, 97

knowledge, 2, 9, 10, 21, 39, 47,
53, 80, 85, 98, 102

language, 53

large families. See family

late marriage. *See* marriage

leisure, 14, 59, 60

liberty, 99

lies, 48, 79

lifestyle, 15, 48, 80

limitations, 18, 65, 94, 96

logical, 20, 70, 73, 75

loss, 17, 36, 37, 57, 61, 67, 71,
84, 87, 95, 98

love. *See* virtue

mainstream, 37

manners, 80

marital dissolution. *See* marriage

marriage: children, 2, 24, 26,
32, 33, 36, 42, 52, 54, 59, 60,
62, 64–68, 72, 73, 75, 76, 78,
79, 81–84, 86, 88, 89,
94–96, 100, 101, 103; communication, 6, 91; early, 50;
ending (divorce), 28, 31, 59,
83, 89, 102; family life, 44,
64, 67, 76–79, 94; general
aspects, 3, 18–20, 23–27,
29–32, 34, 38, 39, 41, 42, 44,
45, 48, 49, 51, 52, 54, 55, 57,
58, 59, 61, 62, 64–67, 69–72,
75, 79–84, 86, 87, 89, 94,
96, 97, 100, 102; husband,
3, 22, 27, 28, 30, 36, 38,
49–51, 54, 56, 59, 62, 69, 71,
72, 75, 78, 81, 83, 87–89, 92,
94, 102; ideals, 1, 3, 4, 11, 12,
18, 41, 42, 48, 61, 63–67, 74,
76, 79–84, 90, 92, 93, 101;
late, 49, 50; marital dissolution, 28; parenthood, 2, 47,
69, 71, 79; partners, 16, 38,
39, 69, 75, 84, 85, 97–99;
spouse, 3, 4, 13, 18, 20, 30,
32, 34, 38, 41, 42, 44–46, 49,
52, 54, 56, 57, 73, 79, 97, 98;
state of, 30, 60, 77, 93; wife,
3, 22, 27, 28, 30, 33, 36, 38,
49–51, 54–56, 59, 62, 63, 69,
72, 75, 76, 78, 79, 81, 83, 84,
88, 92, 102

masculine, 54, 55, 62, 63

match, 14, 17, 32, 29, 31, 37, 49, 60

material, 1, 14, 28, 30, 37, 38, 63, 93

material aspects, 44

material concerns, 87

materialism, 37, 61

matrimony, 30, 60, 77, 93

maturity, 52, 53, 55, 59, 76, 77, 88, 92

means, 12, 34, 42, 54, 56, 57, 61, 76, 81, 84, 88, 95, 100, 101

mechanical, 44, 67

mechanisms: intellectual, 32; mate-choosing, 6; social, 94, 99; spiritual, 65

media, 42, 59

methods, 4, 18, 20, 37, 41, 46, 74, 93

Middle Ages. *See* history

migration, 36, 37, 40, 61, 66, 98, 99

mind, 5, 11, 39, 41

minority, 29–32, 37

mixed, 19, 30–32, 80

model, 42, 64, 67, 79, 84, 92

modern period, 40, 50, 95

modernist, 46, 48

money. *See* financial issues

morality and ethics: ethics, 87, 103; ideals, 1, 3, 4, 11, 12, 18, 41, 42, 48, 61, 63–67, 74, 76, 79–84, 90, 92, 93, 101; morals, 58, 64, 87, 103

mother. *See* family

motherhood, 78, 79, 84

motivations, 1, 2, 43, 69, 101

myth, 70

narrow, 12, 40, 47

nation. *See* government and politics

natural, 1, 9, 38, 60, 65, 72, 76, 77, 91

nature, 3, 4, 7, 19, 26, 33, 47, 48, 63, 65, 71, 79, 90, 91

necessity, 16, 30, 37, 38, 56, 62

need, 1, 2, 5, 6, 27, 37, 39, 45, 48, 65, 67, 68, 74, 75, 79, 86, 92, 94, 98, 101

negotiate, 40

nobility, 42, 62–64, 66

North America, 50

numbers, 76, 82, 83, 94

obligations, 59, 95, 98, 100

obstacle, 60

occult, 65

occupation, 36, 40, 60, 62

opinions, 2, 11, 16–20, 21–23, 26–29, 31, 33, 34, 35–37, 40, 50, 84, 88, 91, 99–102

opportunities, 56, 58, 60, 63, 98

opposite sex, 2, 34, 54, 72

order, 5, 6, 9, 11, 13, 15, 30, 37, 39, 54, 60, 65, 66, 72, 75, 80, 88, 92, 95, 96, 99, 101, 102

origin, 13, 42, 43

over-dependence, 43, 98

parameters, 59

parent, 2, 47, 69, 71

parenthood, 79

parents. *See* family

partners, 5, 13, 37, 39, 51, 53, 54, 58, 69, 75, 85, 97, 99

peasants, 42, 80

penalties, 89, 96

perception, 5, 53, 90

perfect, 1, 10, 38

period, 11, 19, 31, 38, 40, 47, 49, 50, 57, 63, 66, 68, 69, 75, 81, 82, 95, 96

personal sacrifice, 102

personality: differences, 4, 5, 10–12, 15, 27, 28, 57; extroversion, 14; introversion, 14; similarity, 4–8, 11, 12, 13–15, 19, 39, 49–51, 55, 60, 68, 73, 80, 82, 97. *See also* emotions; traits

perspective, 12, 21, 56, 99

phenomenon, 28, 33, 43, 71, 77, 83

planning, 2, 11, 18, 40, 88, 101

political issues. *See* government and politics

popular media, 42

population, 49, 82, 103

possess, 9, 10, 33, 41, 51, 63, 87

poverty. *See* financial issues

powerful, 84, 88, 102

pre-marital relations: attractiveness, 5, 15, 16, 32, 36, 59, 70, 72, 87, 90, 92; celibacy, 80, 84; commitment, 8; courtship, 17, 19, 26, 29, 31, 35, 46, 49, 91, 92, 94; dating, 16–19, 26, 29, 35, 36; opposite sex, 2, 34, 54, 72; single men, 52, 53; single women, 52

preserve, 13, 37, 63, 87

principles, 5, 27, 32, 38, 50, 51, 74, 76, 86, 87, 100

private, 6, 39, 40, 75, 101

processes, 2, 29, 49, 51, 87, 100, 101

proportion, 32, 50, 82, 83

prostitution, 65

protection, 3, 40

prototype, 38, 63, 80

psychology, 2, 7, 37, 60, 64, 65, 70, 74, 75, 77, 87, 90

public, 47, 64–66, 70, 75, 91

purposes, 30, 56

pursuit, 43, 85

qualities, 1, 11, 56, 87, 99

questions, 8, 16–19, 22, 23, 25, 28, 84

race, 7, 8, 13, 17, 25, 26, 30–32, 36, 100

racialism, 48

rank. *See* status

reason, 13–15, 18, 52, 55, 69–71, 77, 88

reasonable, 2, 16, 52

reasoning, 68, 101

reference, 4, 40

reinforcement, 55

relationship: companionate, 14, 57, 73; companionate, 11; complementary, 11; components of, 1; dating, 16, 26; enduring, 91; deeper, 32; intimate, 2, 4, 5, 11, 13, 17, 19, 70; male-female, 4, 8, 46, 56, 72; marital, 3, 34, 72; opposite-sex, 8, 9; relationship dyads, 10; relationship viability, 9, 37; rewarding relationship, 15; same-sex, 7–9; transforming, 2; type of, 5, 11, 34

religion, 8, 17, 60

respect, 10, 16, 28, 44, 47, 67, 83, 95

responsibility, 65, 75, 83

reticence, 37

revolution. *See* government and politics

rewards, 11, 59, 86

rights, 45, 67

risk, 8, 17, 69

romantic, 7, 9, 69

rules, 9, 16, 17, 45, 75, 80, 81, 86, 95

sacrifices, 47, 65, 95

savings. *See* financial issues

scenario, 18, 36, 40, 55, 67, 82

schools and schooling. *See* education and learning

science, 48, 70, 78

secret, 65, 71

security, 65, 67, 68, 71, 73, 83, 90

selfishness, 42, 43, 45, 47, 58, 94, 103

self-centred, 2, 7, 43, 46, 97

servants, 14, 64, 67

sex and sexuality, 2, 7–9, 11, 34, 45, 54, 62, 71, 72, 76

shyness, 48

sibling. *See* family

simplifications, 47, 49, 56, 80, 96, 97

social: action, 67; activity, 54; adjustments, 37; arrangement, 64; background, 8; change, 38; circle, 69, 73, 94; climate, 95; components, 8; context, 30, 91; correction, 88; divisions, 84; duty, 68; entities, 14; environment, 17, 75, 92; exclusion, 32; forces, 18, 50, 101; functions, 6, 17, 29, 95;

gatherings, 6; group, 18, 30; importance, 100; integration, 32; levels, 39; mechanisms, 94, 99; need, 74, 86; norms, 31, 40; obligation, 95, 100; organisation, 93; penalties, 89, 96; policy, 8; precepts, 64; pressures, 55; processes, 2; reaction, 87; relations, 55, 93, 98, 101; roles, 66; situations, 91; stability, 68; standards, 89, 95; struggles, 74; traditions, 61; trends, 40, 102; types, 100; unit, 66

social class. *See* status

society, 3, 4, 8, 30–32, 36, 37, 39, 42, 43, 46, 47, 62, 64–67, 70, 72, 74, 77–79, 83–86, 89, 93, 95–97, 99–101

sophistication, 3, 33

spectrum, 22, 27, 39, 59

spirit, 45, 64, 65

spouse. *See* family

stages, 12, 17–19

status: class, 8, 33, 40, 63, 68, 84, 96; class-orientated, 40; classes, 5, 33, 63, 64, 68, 77, 81, 87; distinction, 8; excep-

tional, 26; exemplary, 42;
lower class, 96; lower
classes, 33, 63; outstanding,
2; rank, 8, 9, 20, 46, 100;
ruling class, 63; social class,
8, 33; social classes, 77, 87;
social position, 67, 96; upper class, 68; upper classes,
81; wealthier classes, 68
strategies, 40, 42, 43, 48, 51,
58
strength, 2, 20, 21, 22, 56, 58,
59
structure, 31, 45, 62, 66, 74,
96, 97
struggle, 1, 32, 37, 49, 66, 67
student. *See* education and
learning
substitution, 71
success, 15, 16, 38, 39, 41, 50,
57, 65
support, 2, 5–7, 30, 36, 40, 43,
44, 74, 75, 83, 84, 89, 98
suspicion, 41, 69
symbols, 41, 77
synchronisation, 6
system, 21, 32, 85, 98, 100

tactics, 40, 98

teachers. See education and
learning
temperament, 6, 9–12, 14, 15,
19, 35, 38, 49, 59, 60
tendency, 33, 35, 51, 71, 81, 91
test of relationship, 9
thought, 41, 48, 60, 64, 66,
70–72, 87, 94, 96
threats, 7, 66, 93
traditional: concept, 49, 83;
concepts, 87, 95; culture,
80; family, 99; idea, 81;
ideal, 41; ideas, 86; standards, 74; times, 92; traditionalism, 58, 61, 74, 90, 97,
99, 101 values, 36, 98; wisdom, 73, 86
traits: differences, 4–6, 8,
10–12, 14, 15, 19, 28, 36, 38,
44, 52, 56, 57, 58, 92, 97, 99,
101–103; general, 4–6, 8–12,
14, 16, 37, 49–51, 56, 63, 70,
90, 91, 95, 97, 103;
heterology, 4, 5, 10–12, 15,
27, 57; heterophily, 4, 28;
homogeneity, 37, 38; homogeneous, 61, 99, 100; ho-
mogenisation, 80, 82;
homology, 4–8, 11, 12, 13–15,

traits (*continued*)
19, 39, 49–51, 55, 60, 68, 73, 97; homophily, 4, 51, 60; similarities, 5, 11, 30, 92; similarity, 4, 6, 7, 10–12, 13–16, 21, 28, 29, 32, 37, 38, 43, 45, 46, 49, 51, 52, 54–56, 60, 74, 88, 91, 102; similitude, 8, 10, 51

truth, 17, 67, 85

type, 5, 11, 14, 29, 31, 33, 34, 46, 55, 63, 70, 71, 98

union, 15, 29, 32, 33, 48, 50, 59, 65, 66, 70, 93

United States, 82

universal, 1, 38, 49

unreasonable, 9, 99

unstable, 84

values, 3, 5, 8, 16, 22, 28, 36, 37, 58, 97–99

variations, 86, 103

variety, 2, 12, 29, 63, 96, 97, 100

viability, 9, 37

Victorian, 69, 95

village, 38, 39

violence, 65, 66

virtue: general, 1, 17, 33, 36, 40, 45, 63, 67, 99; honesty, 40, 63; honour, 67; integrity, 40; love, 2, 3, 7, 11, 12, 15, 30, 41, 42, 45, 61, 66, 69–72, 74–77, 80; true love, 15

warmth, 7, 64

weaknesses, 2, 9, 11, 12, 16, 30, 39, 59, 92, 98

wealth. *See* financial issues

wedlock, 66, 72

well-matched, 17

Western, 8, 16, 33, 37, 38, 42, 43, 49, 58, 61, 63, 74, 75, 78, 82, 90, 94–99, 103

Western culture, 16, 58, 61, 98, 99

Western societies, 8, 37, 38, 43, 97

wholeness, 3, 4, 10, 12, 41, 46, 90

wife. *See* family

willing, 24-26, 30, 38, 39, 52

wish, 21, 29, 69

women, 1, 4, 8, 12, 14, 19, 20, 27, 28, 30, 33, 34, 36, 43, 44, 49–55, 57, 60–70, 72, 73,

74–76, 78–84, 86–89, 90, 91,
94–96, 99

work. *See* career

world, 7, 12, 33, 42, 49, 54, 60,
64, 65, 73, 74, 78, 90,
93–96, 102

worry, 42, 72

wrong, 33, 75, 102

years, 21, 41, 52, 53, 57, 76, 83,
85, 102

yield, 17, 44

young, 7, 9, 45, 51–53, 60, 71,
79

youth, 45, 54